Mediterranean CROCHET

Lyric Books Limited

© 1993 Lyric Books Limited
Central House, 7-8 Ritz Parade, Western Avenue, London W5 3RA, England

ISBN 0 7111 0035 7

Reprinted 1994

Printed in Belgium by
Proost International Book Production

Series Editor: Jenny McIvor
Production Editor: Pauline Moss

CONTENTS

INTRODUCTION

If you enjoy crochet but would like to turn your skills towards something other than making clothes, 'Mediterrranean Crochet' is for you. Taking its influence from the confident style of Southern Europe, the book represents a collection of patterns for decorative items designed to suit both traditional and contemporary interiors.

Clear row-by-row instructions, tables of abbreviations and appealing colour photographs offer a comprehensive approach to choosing from the wide range of projects available. Whether it be the simplicity of a table centre or the more ambitious ideas for bedspreads and cushions, the choices are an inspiration. Each project is rated for its level of intricacy, so that you can be certain which is right as you develop your level of skill. Both the charts and enlargements of each design will ensure that your work is accurate.

This beautiful and informative volume, the second in a series, contains all the design background and professional know-how to help you enjoy the satisfaction of creating wonderful home accessories for yourself.

General Information

Abbreviations

Beg = beginning; **blk(s)** = block(s); **ch** = chain; **dec** = decrease; **dc** = double crochet; **dtr** = double treble; **htr** = half treble; **inc** = increase; **quatr** = quadruple treble; **quintr** = quintuple treble; **rep** = repeat; **sl st** = slip stitch; **sp(s)** = space(s); **st(s)** = stitch(es); **tr** = treble; **ttr** = triple treble; **tog** = together; yo = yarn over.

Special Abbreviations

Tr2tog, tr3tog, tr4tog or tr5tog = work 2, 3, 4 or 5tr into st or sp as indicated leaving last loop of each tr on hook, yo and draw through all the loops on hook.

Dtr2tog, dtr3tog, dtr4tog or dtr5tog = work 2, 3, 4 or 5dtr into st or sp as indicated leaving last loop of each dtr on hook, yo and draw through all the loops on hook.

Ttr2tog, ttr3tog, ttr4tog or ttr5tog = work 2, 3, 4 or 5ttr into st or sp as indicated leaving last loop of each ttr on hook, yo and draw through all the loops on hook.

Quadtr2tog, Quadtr3tog, Quadtr4tog, or Quadtr5tog, = work 2, 3, 4 or 5quadtr into st or sp as indicated leaving last loop of each quadtr on hook, yo and draw through all the loops on hook.

Picot = work 3ch, work 1dc into first of these ch.

When joining with a picot, work as follows: 1ch, sl st into picot, st or arch as indicated, 1ch, work 1dc into first of these ch.

▉ **= 1 block (blk)** = work 4tr for first blk, then 3tr for each additional blk.

☐ **=1 space (sp)** = work 1tr, 2ch, 1tr for first sp, then 2ch, 1tr for each additional sp.

To inc 1 blk at beg of row = make 5ch, work 1tr into 4th ch from hook, 1tr into next ch, 1tr into next tr. Work 3 more ch (3 more tr) for each additional blk to be increased.

To inc 1 blk at end of row = work to last tr, yo, insert crochet hook into last tr and draw loop through, yo and through 1 loop on hook (1 base ch made), [yo and through 2 loops on hook] twice, *yo, insert hook into last base ch made and draw loop through, yo and through 1 loop on hook (another base ch made), [yo and through 2 loops on hook] twice, rep from * twice more - work from * 3 times more for each additional blk to be increased.

To dec 1 blk at beg of row = Sl st into each of first 4tr - sl st into 3 more tr for each additional blk to be decreased.

To dec 1 blk at end of row = work to last 3tr, turn - work 3tr less for each additional blk to be decreased.

Notes

Repeat instructions following an asterisk, (*), as many more times as specified in addition to the original.

Repeat instructions in square brackets, [ ], as many times as specified.

To make counting easier when making a large number of chain, tie a length of contrasting yarn into every 20th or 50th ch made.

Washing and Pressing Instructions

Crochet items should not be washed when work is still in progress. The assembled article should be washed on completion.

Make a warm lather of pure soap flakes and wash in the usual way, either by hand or washing machine. If required, the article may be spin-dried until it is damp, or left until it is half dry. Place a piece of paper, either plain white or squared on top of a clean, flat surface. Draw the shape of the finished article onto the paper, using a ruler and set square for squares and rectangles and a

pair of compasses for circles. Using rustless pins, pin the crochet onto the pencilled shape, taking care not to strain the crochet. Pin out the general shape first, then finish by pinning each picot, arch or space into position.

Special points to note carefully when pinning out are: -

1) When pinning arches, make sure the pin is in the centre of each loop to form balanced lines.

2) When pinning scallops, make all the scallops the same size and regularly curved.

3) Pull out all picots.

4) Where there are flowers, pull out each petal in position.

5) When pinning filet crochet, make sure that the spaces and blocks are square and that all edges are even and straight.

If the crochet requires to be slightly stiffened, use a solution of starch - 1 dessertspoonful to ½ litre hot water, and dab lightly over the article. Raise the crochet up off the paper to prevent it sticking as it dries. When dry, remove the pins and press the article lightly with a hot iron.

Materials

Throughout this publication we have recommended products by Coats Patons Crafts. This, however, is only a suggestion and any equivalent yarn, needle or sewing thread of the correct gauge may be substituted if preferred.

Yarn Equivalent	
U.K.	**Australia**
Opera 5	Pellicano
Opera 20	Coats Mercer Crochet Cotton tkt 20
Opera 30	Coats Mercer Crochet Cotton tkt 30
Musica 5	Pellicano
Musica 8	South Maid
Sylko Sewing Thread	Duet sewing thread

SUNSHINE YELLOW

Trim any cloth or perhaps your kitchen shelves with this intricate edging of bells and stars.

This delicate tablecloth is deceptively simple to make. The fans and stars are the perfect companion for the trimming opposite.

1

Flower Edging

★★★

Materials

Coats Patons Opera No. 20 Crochet Cotton Shade 500 - 50 grams

1.00mm Milward Steel Crochet Hook

First Flower

Make 9ch, join into a ring with a sl st.

1st round: 3ch, into ring work 1tr, 1 picot (see Special Abbreviations on page 5), 1ch, [tr2tog into ring, 1 picot, 1ch] 7 times, sl st into 3rd of 3ch.

2nd round: Sl st into first sp, 8ch (count as 1tr, 5ch), [1tr into next sp, 5ch] 7 times, sl st into 3rd of 8ch.

3rd round: Sl st into first sp, [1dc, 1htr, 1tr, 3dtr, 1tr, 1htr, 1dc] into same sp as last sl st, 3ch, *[1dc, 1htr, 1tr, 3dtr, 1tr, 1htr, 1dc] into next sp, 3ch; rep from * 6 times, sl st into first dc. 8 petals.

4th round: Sl st into first dtr of first petal, 1dc into next dtr, *5ch, [1tr, 3ch, 1tr] into 3ch arch, 5ch, 1dc into centre dtr of next petal; rep from * 6 times, 5ch, [1tr, 3ch, 1tr] into last 3ch arch, 3ch, sl st into first dc.

5th round: Sl st into centre of first 5ch arch, 1dc into same arch, 5ch, 1dc into next tr, 3ch, 1dc into next 3ch arch, 3ch, 1dc into next tr, *5ch, [1dc into next 5ch arch, 5ch] twice, 1dc into next tr, 3ch, 1dc into next 3ch arch, 3ch, 1dc into next tr; rep from * 6 times more, 5ch, 1dc into next 5ch arch, 5ch, sl st into first dc.

6th round: Sl st into centre of first 5ch arch, 1dc into same arch, 5ch, 1dc into next 5ch arch, 3ch, into next 5ch arch work [dtr3tog, 3ch, dtr3tog], *3ch, 1dc into next 5ch arch, 5ch, 1dc into next 5ch arch, 3ch, into next 5ch arch work [dtr3tog, 3ch, dtr3tog]; rep from * 6 times more, 3ch, sl st into first dc.

Fasten off. 8 double cluster petals.

Second Flower

Work first 5 rounds as given for First Flower.

6th round: Sl st into centre of first 5ch arch, 1dc into same arch, 5ch, 1dc into next 5ch arch, 3ch, *into next 5ch arch work [dtr3tog, 1 joining picot into 3ch arch of a petal of previous flower, dtr3tog], 3ch, 1dc into next 5ch arch, 5ch, 1dc into next 5ch arch, 3ch; rep from * once more, then complete round as for first flower.

Make 6 more flowers joining each to the previous flower as before to form a strip.

Linking Motifs

Make 8ch, join into a ring with a sl st.

3ch, 1tr into ring, 1 picot, 1ch, tr2tog into ring, 1dtr into 3rd free 3ch arch of first left hand flower from the left of the join with next flower, 1ch, tr2tog, into ring, 1tr into next 5ch arch of flower, 1ch, tr2tog into ring, 1htr into next 3ch arch of flower, 1ch, tr2tog 1htr into corresponding 3ch arch of next flower, 1ch, tr2tog into ring, 1tr into next 5ch arch of flower, 1ch, tr2tog into ring, 1dtr into next 3ch arch of flower, 1ch, tr2tog, 1 picot, 1ch, sl st into first tr.

Fasten off.

Work 6 linking motifs to join the remaining flowers at the top edge.

Top Edging

With right side facing rejoin yarn to 3ch arch of 3rd petal of first flower to the right of joining motif and work as follows:

1st row: 18ch (count as 1quintr, 11ch), 1dc into centre arch of next petal, 2ch, 1dc into next 3ch arch at left of same petal, 8ch, 1dc into 3ch arch at right of next petal, 2ch, 1dc into centre arch of petal, *8ch, 1dc into first picot of joining motif, 2ch, 1dc into next picot, 8ch, 1dc into centre arch of first free petal on next flower, 2ch, 1dc into 3ch arch at

left of petal, 8ch, 1dc into 3ch arch at right of next petal, 2ch, 1dc into centre arch of petal; rep from * to last flower, 11ch, 1quintr into centre arch of next petal on last flower, turn.

2nd row: 5ch (count as 1tr, 2ch), miss 2 sts, *1tr into next st, miss 2 sts; rep from * to last 8ch, 1tr into next ch, turn.
3rd row: Work [2dc, 3ch, 2dc] into each 2ch sp to end.

Fasten off.

Lower Edging

1st row: *11ch, 1ttr into top of first cluster of next petal, 5ch, 1dtr into next cluster, 11ch, 1dtr into first cluster of next petal, turn, work [1dc, 1htr, 11tr, 1htr, 1dc] over last 11ch, turn, 17ch, 1dc into next dtr, turn, work [1dc, 1htr, 21tr, 1htr, 1dc] over last 17ch, 1dc into next dtr, 4ch, 1tr into next dtr, turn, 9ch, miss 8 sts on last arch, 1dtr into next tr, 14ch, miss 8tr, 1dtr into next tr, 9ch, [1dtr, 3ch, 1quadtr] into next dtr, 1ttr into next cluster, 11ch, 1dc into st joining 2 flowers; rep from * to end placing last dc into last free centre arch of petal, turn.

Working the triangle motifs between each flower, continue as follows:

Work 15dc into first 11ch arch, 5dc into next 3ch arch, 15dc into next 9ch arch, 30dc into next 14ch arch, *15dc into next 9ch arch, 5dc into next 3ch arch, 15dc into next 11ch arch, 5dc into next 11ch arch (2nd side of triangle), turn, 4ch, miss 4dc on first side of triangle, 1dc into next dc, sl st into next dc, turn, 5dc into 4ch arch, 5dc into same 11ch arch on 2nd side of triangle, turn, 4ch, miss 2dc on arch on 5dc arch, 1tr into next dc, 4ch, miss 3dc on first side of triangle, 1dc into next dc, sl st into next dc, turn, 5dc into each of the 2 arches, 5dc into same arch on second side of triangle as before, turn, 4ch, [1tr into centre dc of next arch, 4ch] twice, miss 3dc, 1dc into next dc, sl st into next dc, turn, 5dc into each of the 3 arches, 5dc into next arch, turn, 4ch, [1tr into centre dc of next arch, 4ch] 3 times, miss 3dc, 1dc into next dc, sl st into next dc, turn, 5dc into each of the 4 arches, 5dc into next 9ch arch, turn, 4ch, [1tr into centre dc of next arch, 4ch] 4 times, miss 3dc, 1dc into next dc, sl st into next dc, turn, 5dc into each of the 5 arches, 5dc into same 9ch arch as before, turn, 4ch, [1tr into centre dc of next arch, 4ch] 5 times, miss 3dc, 1dc into next dc, sl st into next dc, turn, 5dc into each of the 6 arches, turn, 5dc into same 9ch arch as before, turn, 4ch, [1tr into centre dc of next arch, 4ch] 6 times, miss 3dc, 1dc into next dc, sl st into next dc, turn, 5dc into each of the 7 arches, 5dc into next 14ch arch, turn, 4ch, [1tr into

centre dc of next arch, 4ch] 7 times, miss 3dc, 1dc into next dc, sl st into next dc, turn, 5dc into each of the 8 arches, 5dc into same arch as before, turn, 4ch, [1tr into centre dc of next arch, 4ch] 8 times, miss 3dc, 1dc into next dc, sl st into next dc, turn, 5dc into each of the 9 arches, 5dc into same arch as before, turn, 4ch, [1tr into centre dc of next arch, 4ch] 9 times, miss 3dc, 1dc into next dc, sl st into next dc, turn, into each of the 10 arches work [3dc, 3ch, 3dc], 15dc into same 14ch arch as before; rep from * 6 times more, then work 15dc into next 9ch arch, 5dc into next 3ch arch, and 15dc into last 11ch arch, sl st into first dc.

Fasten off.

— ◆ —

2
Small Tablecloth
✪✪

Materials

Coats Patons Opera No. 20 Crochet Cotton Shade 500 - 400 grams
1.00mm Milward Steel Crochet Hook

Note

The Tablecloth is made up of 8 panels of 10 square motifs. The motifs are worked separately and connected on the last round to form the panel. The panels are then joined together and a final edging applied.

First Panel

First Square

Make 4ch, join into a ring with a sl st.

1st round: 3ch (count as 1tr), 1 picot (see Special Abbreviations on page 5) into ring, work [1tr, 1 picot] 7 times, sl st into 3rd of 3ch. (8 sps).

2nd round: 7ch (count as 1tr, 4ch), *1tr into next tr, 4ch; rep from * to end, sl st into 3rd of 4ch.

3rd round: 3ch (count as 1tr), *5tr into 4chsp, 1tr into next tr; rep from * to end omitting 1tr at end of last rep, sl st into 3rd of 3ch. 48 tr.

4th round: 3ch, 1tr into same st as last sl st, *1tr into each of next 9tr, 2tr into next tr, 2ch, miss 1tr, 2tr into next tr, 1tr into each of next 4tr, 2ch, miss 1tr, 1tr into each of next 4tr, 2tr into next tr, 2ch, miss 1tr*, 2tr into next tr; rep from * to * once more, sl st into 3rd of 3ch.

Working 1tr into each tr of previous round unless otherwise indicated, continue as follows.

5th round: 3ch, 1tr into same st as last st st, *11tr, 2tr into next st, 3ch, 2tr into next st, 5tr, 3ch, 5tr, 2tr into next st, 3ch*, 2tr into next st; rep from * to * once, sl st into 3rd of 3ch.

6th round: 3ch, 1tr into same st as last st st, *13tr, 2tr into next st, 5ch, 2tr into next st, 6tr, 3ch, 6tr, 2tr into next st, 3ch, *2tr into next st; rep from * to * once, sl st into 3rd of 3ch.

7th round: 3ch, 1tr into same st as last sl st, *7tr, 3ch, miss 1tr, 7tr, 2tr into next tr, 2ch, [2tr, 3ch, 2tr] into next sp (for corner), 2ch, 2tr into next tr, 7tr, 4ch, 7tr, 2tr into next tr, 2ch, [2tr, 3ch, 2tr] into next sp, 2ch*, 2tr into next tr; rep from * to * once, sl st into 3rd of 3ch.

8th round: 3ch, 1tr into same st as last sl st, *7tr, 4ch, 1dc into next sp, 4ch, miss 1tr, 7tr, 2tr into next tr, 3ch, miss 1 sp, [2tr, 3ch, 2tr] into corner sp, 3ch, 2tr into next tr; rep from * 3 times omitting 2tr at end of last rep, sl st into 3rd of 3ch.

9th round: 3ch, miss first st, 7tr, * [4ch, 1dc in next sp] twice, 4ch, miss 1st, 8tr, 4ch, miss 1 sp, [2tr, 3ch, 2tr] into next sp, 4ch, 8tr; rep from * 3 times, omitting 8tr at end of last rep, sl st into 3rd of 3ch.

10th round: 3ch, miss first st, 6tr, *[4ch, 1dc into next sp] 3 times, 4ch, miss 1st, 7tr, 3ch, 1dc into sp, 4ch, [2tr, 3ch, 2tr] into next sp, 4ch, 1dc into next sp, 3ch, 7tr; rep from * 3 times omitting 7tr at end of last rep, sl st into 3rd of 3ch.

11th round: Sl st into next st, 3ch (count as 1tr), 4tr, *[4ch, 1dc into next sp] 4 times, 4ch, miss 1st, 5tr, [4ch, 1dc into sp] twice, 4ch, [2tr, 3ch, 2tr] into next sp, 4ch, 1dc into next sp, 3ch, 5tr; rep from * 3 times omitting 5tr at end of last rep, sl st into 3rd of 3ch.

12th round: Sl st into next st, tr2tog over next 2sts, 3ch, *[4ch, 1dc into next sp] 5 times, 4ch, miss 1st, tr3tog, [4ch, 1dc into sp] 3 times, 4ch ★, [2tr, 3ch, 2tr] into next sp, [4ch, 1dc into next sp] 3 times, 4ch, miss 1st, tr3tog; rep from * 3 times omitting tr3tog at end of last rep, sl st into 3rd of 3ch.

Fasten off.

Subsequent Squares

Work as first square to ★ then continue as follows:

2tr into next sp, 1ch, 1dc into corresponding sp of previous square, 1ch, 2tr, *2ch, 1dc into corresponding sp of previous square, 2ch; rep from * to next corner, into corner sp work 2tr, 1ch, 1dc into corresponding sp of previous square, 1ch, 2tr, then complete 12th round.

Work 8 more squares in the same way.

Inner Edging

Rejoin yarn to one corner of panel and work along long sides as follows:

1st row: 1dc into corner sp, *3ch, 1dc in next sp; rep from * to end, turn.

2nd row: 1ch, work 4dc into each sp to end, turn.

3rd row: 4ch (count as 1tr, 1ch), miss first 2dc, *1tr, 1ch, miss 1dc; rep from * to last dc, 1tr into last dc, turn.

4th row: 1ch, 1dc into first tr, *8ch, miss 2sp, 1dc into next sp; rep from * to end. Fasten off.

Second Panel

Work as First Panel to 4th row of edging, then work 4th row of edging joining panel to the first one as follows: 1dc into first tr, *4ch, 1dc into corresponding sp of previous panel, 4ch, miss 2sp on 2nd panel, 1dc into next sp; rep from * to end.

Work 5 more panels as Second Panel, then work 1 more panel working edging on one side only to join to 5th panel.

Outer Edging

Starting at corner sp of one shorter edge of tablecloth, rejoin yarn and work as follows:

1st round: ★ 3dc into corner sp, [3ch, 1dc into next sp] 17 times, 3ch, 1tr into join between 2 panels, *[3ch 1dc into next sp] 20 times, 3ch, 1tr into join between 2 panels; rep from * 5 times, [3ch, 1dc into next sp] 17 times, 3ch, 3dc into next sp for corner, ** 3ch, 1dc into next sp; rep from ** to next corner, 3ch; rep from * once, sl st into first dc.

2nd round: *1dc into each of 3dc at corner, ** 4dc into next sp; rep from ** to next corner; rep from * 3 times, sl st into first dc.

3rd round: 4ch (count as 1tr, 1ch), [1tr, 1ch, 1tr] into corner st, ★ *1ch, miss 1st, 1tr into next dc; rep from * to next corner, [1ch 1tr] 3 times into corner st; rep from ★ to end, sl st into 3rd of 4ch.

4th round: Sl st into first sp, 4ch, *[1dtr, 1 picot] 3 times and 1dtr into next sp, 4ch, miss 1sp, 1dc into next sp, 4ch, miss 2sp; rep from * to end, sl st into first sl st.

Fasten off.

3
Large Pine Cone Doily
✪✪

Materials

Coats Patons Musica No. 5 Crochet Cotton Shade 500 - 50 grams

1.75mm Milward Steel Crochet Hook.

To Make

Make 8ch, join into a ring with a sl st.

1st round: 3ch (count as 1tr), work 11tr into ring, sl st into 3rd of 3ch.

2nd round: 3ch, 1tr into same st as last sl st, *2tr in next st; rep from * to end, sl st into 3rd of 3ch.

3rd round: 7ch (count as 1tr, 4ch), miss next tr, *1tr into next tr, 4ch, miss next tr; rep from * to end, sl st into 3rd of 7ch. 12 sps.

4th round: 3ch, *6tr into 4chsp, 1tr into next tr; rep from * to end omitting 1tr at end of last rep, sl st into 3rd of 3ch. 84 tr.

5th round: 3ch (count as 1tr), 1tr into each tr to end, sl st into 3rd of 3ch.

6th round: 2ch, tr2tog over next 2tr, *1tr into each of next 3tr, tr2tog over next 2tr, 2ch, tr2tog; rep from * to end of last rep, sl st into top of first tr2tog.

7th round: 3ch (count as 1tr), 1tr into each of next 2tr, *tr2tog over next 2tr, 2ch, 1tr into 2chsp, 2ch, 1tr into each

This impressive centre piece
proves that doilies can be both
traditional yet fashionable. With
its star and Pine-cone theme it will
look great on your table from
breakfast till supper.

20th round: *2tr, 3ch, [1tr, 1ch in next 1chsp] 4 times, 2ch, miss 1tr, 2tr, 1ch, 2tr, 2ch, 7tr in next sp, 2ch, 2tr, 1ch; rep from * to end, sl st into 3rd of 3ch.

21st round: *2tr, 3ch, [1tr, 1ch into next 1chsp] 3 times, 2ch, miss 1tr, 2tr, 1ch, 2tr, 2ch, [1tr, 1ch between next 2tr] 6 times, 1ch, miss 2ch, 2tr, 1ch, rep from * to end, sl st into 3rd of 3ch.

22nd round: *2tr, 3ch, [1tr, 1ch into next 1chsp] twice, 2ch, miss 1tr, 2tr, 1ch, 2tr, 2ch, [1tr 1ch between next 2tr] 5 times, 1ch, miss 1tr, 2tr, 1ch; rep from * to end, sl st into 3rd of 3ch.

23rd round: *2tr, 3ch, [1tr, 1ch] into next 1chsp, 3ch, miss 1tr, 2tr, 1ch, 2tr, 2ch, [1tr 1ch between next 2tr] 4 times, 1ch, 2tr, 1ch; rep from * to end, sl st into 3rd of 3ch.

24th round: *2tr, 2ch, miss 2sp, 2tr, 1ch, 2tr, 3ch, [1tr, 1ch between next 2tr] 3 times, 2ch, miss 1tr, 2tr, 1ch; rep from * to end, sl st into 3rd of 3ch.

25th round: *2tr, 3tr into next sp, 2tr, 1ch, 2tr, 4ch, [1tr, 1ch between next 2tr] twice, 3ch, miss 1tr, 2tr, 1ch; rep from * to end, sl st into 3rd of 3ch.

26th round: *2tr, 4ch, miss 3st, 2tr, 1ch, 2tr, 5ch, 1tr into 1chsp, 5ch, miss 1tr, 2tr, 1ch, rep from * to end, sl st into 3rd of 3ch.

27th round: *2tr, 1ch, [1dtr, 1ch, 1dtr, 2ch, 1dtr, 1ch, 1dtr] into next chsp, 1ch, 2tr, 1ch, 2tr, 1ch, [2tr, 1ch] twice into each of next 2sp, 2tr, 1ch; rep from * to end, sl st into 3rd of 3ch.

Scallop Edge

Each scallop is worked separately.

1st row: Turn work (wrong side) and sl st into last tr made, [2ch, 1dtr into next sp] twice, 2ch, 3dtr into next sp, [2ch, 1dtr into next sp] twice, 2ch, miss 2tr, sl st into next 3 sts, turn.

2nd row: [3ch, 1dtr into next sp] twice, 3ch, 2dtr into next sp, 1dtr into each of next 3 sts, 2dtr into next sp, [3ch, 1dtr into next sp] twice, 3ch, miss 1tr, sl st into next 3 sts, turn.

3rd row: [3ch, 1dtr into next sp] 3 times, 1dtr into each of next 7 sts, [1dtr 3ch into next sp] 3 times, miss 2tr, sl st into next 3 sts, turn.

4th row: [3ch, 1dtr into next sp] 3 times, [3ch, miss 2 sts, 1dtr into next st] twice, [3ch, 1dtr in next sp] 3 times, 3ch, miss 1tr, sl st in next sp.

Fasten off.

Work the remaining 11 scallops in the same way. With wrong side facing, start each scallop by rejoining yarn into 6th free tr following the previous scallop.

---

of next 3sts; rep from * to end omitting 3tr at end of last rep, sl st into 3rd of 3ch.

8th round: *[Tr2tog over 2sts] twice, [2ch, 1tr into 2chsp] twice, 2ch; rep from * to end, sl st into first tr2tog.

9th round: *Tr2tog over 2sts, [2ch, 1tr into 2chsp] 3 times, 2ch; rep from * to end, sl st into first tr2tog.

10th round: Sl st into first sp, 5ch (count as 1tr, 2ch), *1tr into next sp, 2ch; rep from * to end, sl st into 3rd of 5ch.

11th round: Sl st into first sp, 6ch (count as 1tr, 3ch), *1tr into next sp, 3ch; rep from * to end, sl st into 3rd of 6ch.

12th round: 3ch, *4tr into sp, 1tr into next tr; rep from * to end omitting 1tr at end of last rep, sl st into 3rd of 3ch.

13th round: 3ch, 1tr into each of next 3tr, *2ch, miss 1st, 1tr into each of next 4tr, 3ch, miss 1st, 1tr into each of next 4tr, 2ch, miss 1st, 1tr into each of next 9tr; rep from * to end omitting 4tr at end of last rep, sl st into 3rd of 3ch.

14th round: 3ch, 1tr into next tr *4ch, 9dtr into next 3chsp, 4ch, miss 2chsp and 2tr, 1tr into each of next 2tr, 2ch, miss 1tr, 1tr into each of next 2tr; rep from * to end, omitting 2tr at end of last rep, sl st into 3rd of 3ch.

15th round: 3ch, 1tr into next tr, *3ch, [1tr, 1ch into next dtr] 9 times, 2ch, 1tr into each of next 2tr, 1ch, 1tr into each of next 2tr; rep from * to end, omitting 2tr at end of last rep, sl st into 3rd of 3ch.

16th round: 3ch, 1tr into next tr, *3ch, [1tr, 1ch into next 1chsp] 8 times, 2ch, miss 1tr, 1tr into each of next 2tr, 1ch, 1tr into each of next 2tr; rep from * to end, omitting 2tr at end of last rep, sl st into 3rd of 3ch.

17th round: 3ch, 1tr into next tr, *3ch, [1tr, 1ch into next 1chsp] 7 times, 2ch, miss 1tr, 1tr into each of next 2tr, 1ch, 1tr into each of next 2tr; rep from * to end, omitting 2tr at end of last rep, sl st into 3rd of 3ch.

18th round: 3ch, 1tr into next tr, *4ch, [1tr, 1ch into next 1chsp] 6 times, 3ch, miss 1tr, 1tr into each of next 2tr, 2tr into next sp, 1tr into each of next 2tr; rep from * to end, omitting 2tr at end of last rep, sl st into 3rd of 3ch.

Continuing to work first tr of each round as 3ch and each tr into tr of previous round unless otherwise indicated, continue as follows:

19th round: *2tr, 3ch, [1tr, 1ch into next 1chsp] 5 times, 2ch, miss 1tr, 2tr, 1ch, 2tr in next st, 3ch, 2tr into next st, 2tr, 1ch; rep from * to end, sl st into 3rd of 3ch.

4

Snowflake Doily

✪

Materials

Coats Patons Musica No. 5 Crochet Cotton Shade 500 - 50 grams

1.75mm Milward Steel Crochet Hook

To Make

Make 10ch, join into a ring with a sl st.

1st round: 3ch (count as 1tr), work 23tr into ring, sl st into 3rd of 3ch.

2nd round: 12ch, miss 2tr, *1ttr into next st, 8ch, miss 2tr, rep from * 6 times, sl st into 4th of 12ch.

3rd round: Sl st into first chsp, 4ch (count as 1dtr), 9dtr in same sp as sl st, *10dtr into next sp; rep from * 6 times, sl st into 4th of 4ch.

4th round: 4ch (count as 1dtr), miss first st, 1dtr into each of next 9dtr, 1ch, * 1dtr into each of next 10dtr, 1ch; rep from * 6 times, sl st into 4th of 4ch.

5th round: 4ch, 9dtr, 3ch, *10dtr, 3ch; rep from * 6 times, sl st into 4th of 4ch.

6th round: 4ch, 9dtr, 5ch, *10dtr, 5ch; rep from * 6 times, sl st into 4th of 4ch.

7th round: 4ch, 9dtr, 7ch, *10dtr, 7ch; rep from * 6 times, sl st into 4th of 4ch.

8th round: 4ch, 9dtr, 9ch, *10dtr, 9ch; rep from * 6 times, sl st into 4th of 4ch.

9th round: 4ch, dtr4tog over next 4sts, 9ch, dtr5tog over next 5sts, 7ch, 1dc into 9chsp, 7ch, *dtr5tog over next 5sts, 9ch, dtr5tog over next 5sts, 7ch, 1dc into 9chsp, 7ch; rep from * 6 times, sl st into 4th of 4ch.

10th round: Sl st into first sp, 4ch, 20dtr in same space as last sl st, 5ch, 1dc into next dc, 5ch, *21dtr into 9chsp, 5ch, 1dc into next dc, 5ch; rep from * 6 times, sl st into 4th of 4ch.

11th round: 5ch (count as 1dtr, 1ch), [1dtr into next dtr, 1ch] 20 times, 2ch, 1dc into next dc, 3ch, * [1dtr into next dtr, 1ch] 21 times, 2ch, 1dc into next dc, 3ch; rep from * 6 times, sl st into 4th of 5ch.

12th round: Working first dc into same st as last sl st continue as follows: *1dc into next dtr, [4ch, dtr3tog over next 3dtr, 1 picot (see Special Abbreviations on page 5), 4ch, sl st into next dtr] 5 times, 3ch, 1dc into dc, 3ch; rep from * 7 times, sl st into first dc.

Fasten off.

TIP

When ironing crochet with loops, place it on a smooth flannel and pin it, making sure a pin is placed in the middle of every loop. If there are any scallops, it is important to check that each one of them is of the same size with a regular bend. If there are any picots, these should be pinned one by one.

5

Rose Tablemat

✪✪✪✪

Materials

Coats Patons Opera No. 20 Crochet Cotton Shade 500 - 100 grams

1.00mm Milward Steel Crochet Hook
1 reel Sylko Sewing Thread

1 sewing needle

35 cm x 20 cm piece of white linen

Note

The long borders of the pattern are formed by 13 large roses and 2 small roses which are worked separately and then joined together forming 2 rows (the first one of 9 roses and the second one of 6 roses).

Outer Row of Roses

First Large Rose

Make 8ch, join into a ring with a sl st.

1st round: 6ch (count as 1tr, 3ch), into ring work [1tr, 3ch] 5 times, sl st into 3rd of 6ch.

2nd round: [1dc, 3htr, 1dc] into each arch to end, sl st into first dc.

3rd round: 1dc into same st as last sl st, 5ch, [miss 4 sts, 1dc into next dc, 5ch] 5 times, sl st into first dc.

4th round: [1dc, 1htr, 3tr, 1htr, 1dc] into each arch to end, sl st into first dc.

4

Bold and striking, this doily's looks won't sacrifice impact for simplicity.

The flowers on your table don't always have to be fresh! Crocheted Irish roses on a plain white linen table mat change something unexceptional into an out of the ordinary piece worthy of any table.

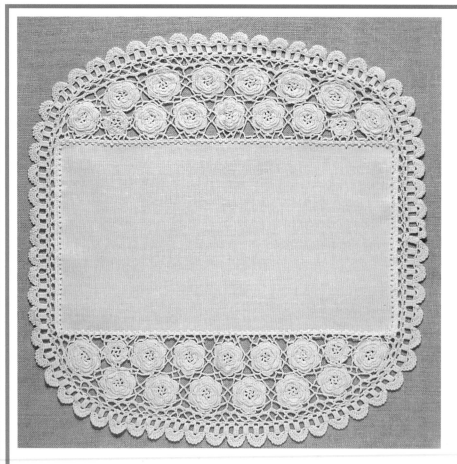

arch of next rose; rep from * to end of row, [3ch, 1htr into next arch] twice, 3ch, [1dtr 3ch 1dtr] into next arch, 8ch, 1tr into stem of last dtr worked, [5ch, 1dc into next arch] 3 times, 5ch, 1tr into next arch, 5ch, ** 1dtr into joining dc between the 2 roses, 5ch, 1tr into next arch, [5ch, 1dc into next arch] twice, 5ch, 1tr into next arch, 5ch, rep from ** 5 times more, 1dtr into joining dc between 2 roses, 5ch, 1tr into next arch, [5ch, 1dc into next arch] 3 times, 5ch, 1tr into stem of first dtr of round, 8ch, sl st into joining sl st.

2nd round: [3dc into next arch, 1 picot (see Special Abbreviations on page 5)] 53 times, *[3dc, 3ch, 3dc] into 5chsp; rep from * to end, sl st into first dc.

Fasten off.

Work another piece the same from ★

Side Inner Border (Make 2)

Make 113ch and work 1dc into 2nd ch from hook, 1dc into each of next 2ch, 1 picot, *1dc into each of next 3ch, 1 picot; rep from * to last ch, work 3dc into last ch, do not turn but work along other side of starting ch as follows: miss first ch, work *1dc into each of next 6ch, 1 picot; rep from * to end.

Fasten off.

Outside Final Edging

Make 14ch.

1st row: Work 1tr into 6th ch from hook, 1tr into each of next 5ch, 2ch, miss 2ch, 1tr into last ch, turn.

2nd row: 3ch (count as 1tr), 2tr into first sp, 6ch, miss 6tr, 1tr into next ch, turn.

3rd row: 5ch, miss first tr, 1tr into each of next 6ch, 2ch, miss 2tr, 1tr into 3rd of 3ch, turn.

4th row: 3ch, 2tr into first sp, 6ch, miss 6st, 1tr in next ch, [1ch, 1tr into 5chsp] 9 times, 1ch, 1dc into 5chsp 3 rows below, turn.

5th row: [3ch, 1dc into next chsp] 10 times, 3ch, 1tr into each of next 6ch, 2ch, miss 2tr, 1tr into 3rd of 3ch, turn.

Rep 2nd to 5th rows inclusive 61 times, then 2nd to 4th rows once more.

Fasten off.

Join first and last rows to form a circle, taking care not to twist work.

Making Up

Make a deep zig-zag all around the fabric and sew the two borders of roses to the long sides leaving the picots free on the fabric edge.

5th round: 1dc into same st as last sl st, 7ch, [miss 6sts, 1dc into next dc, 7ch] 5 times, sl st into first dc.

6th round: [1dc, 1htr, 5tr, 1htr, 1dc] into each arch to end, sl st into first dc.

7th round: 1dc into same st as last sl st, 9ch [miss 8 sts, 1dc into next dc, 9ch] 5 times, sl st into first dc.

8th round: [1dc, 1htr, 7tr, 1htr, 1dc] into each arch to end, sl st into first dc.

9th round: 1dc into same st as last sl st * 7ch, miss 4sts, 1dc into next tr, 7ch, miss 5 sts, 1dc into next dc; rep from * 5 times more omitting 1dc at end of last rep, sl st into first dc.

Fasten off.

Second Large Rose

Work first 8 rounds as given for First Large Rose.

9th round: (Joining round): 1dc into same st as last sl st, *7ch, miss 4 sts, 1dc into next tr, 7ch, miss 5 sts, 1dc into next dc, 3ch, 1dc into a corresponding 7ch arch of first rose, 3ch, miss 4 sts on 2nd rose, 1dc into next dc, 3ch, 1dc into next 7ch arch of first rose, 3ch, miss 5 sts, 1dc into next dc on 2nd rose, then complete round as for first rose.

Work 6 more Large Roses, joining them in a row as before, thus leaving 4 free arches at each side of joins.

Inner Row of Roses
Small Rose

Work first 4 rounds as given for First Large Rose, then, joining it to first 2 large roses of Outer Row in the same way as the large roses as shown on photograph, work the 5th round as follows: 1dc into same st as last sl st, 7ch, miss 2 sts, 1dc into next tr, 7ch, miss 3 sts, 1dc into next dc, 3ch, 1dc into 2nd free arch of 2nd rose on outer row at right of joining arch with first rose, 3ch, miss 3 sts on small rose, 1dc into next dc, continue in this way joining the small rose to next arch on first rose, then to first 2 free arches of 2nd rose and complete the round.

Work 5 more Large Roses and 1 more Small Rose joining them together in a row and to the 8 Large Roses of Outer Row as illustrated.

Inner Edging

With right side facing, rejoin yarn with a sl st into 4th free loop of First Large Rose of Outer Row before the join with the First Small Rose and work as follows:

1st round: 7ch (count as 1dtr, 3ch), 1dtr into same arch as sl st, *[3ch, 1htr into next sp] twice, 3ch, [1dtr, 3ch, 1dtr] into next loop, 5ch, 1tr into stem of last dtr worked, turn, sl st into next 2ch, turn, [1dtr, 3ch, 1dtr] into first free

Sew the 2 side inner borders to the short sides in the same way matching the picots.

Now join the final edging on all 4 sides working into all the 3chsp and picots as follows:

*1dc into 3chsp or into a picot, 3ch, turn, 1dc into stem of tr of final edging, 3ch, turn; rep from * until all spaces and picots have been joined to the tr stems of final edging. (Note: miss 1tr of final edging at points of connection).

Fasten off.

6

Striped Edging

Materials

Coats Patons Opera No. 20 Crochet Cotton Shade 500 - 100 grams

1.00mm Milward Steel Crochet Hook

To Make

1st row: Make 77ch, 1tr into 8th ch from hook, *2ch, miss 2ch, 1tr into next ch; rep from * to end, turn. 73 sts.

2nd row: 3ch (count as 1tr), miss first tr, 1tr into each of next 3sts, [2ch, 1tr into next tr] twice, *11ch, miss 11 sts, 1tr into next st, 2ch, miss 2ch, 1tr into each of next 4 sts 2ch, miss 2ch, 1tr into next st; rep from * once, 11ch, miss 11sts, [1tr into next tr, 2ch] twice, 1tr into each of next 3 sts 1tr into 5th of 7ch, turn.

3rd row: 3ch, miss first st, 1tr into each of next 3 sts, [2ch, 1tr into next tr] twice, *11tr into 11chsp, [1tr into next tr, 2ch] 3 times, 1tr into next tr; rep from * once, 11tr into 11chsp, [1tr into next tr, 2ch] twice, 1tr into each of next 3tr, 1tr into 3rd of 3ch, turn.

4th row: As 2nd row.

5th row: As 3rd row.

6th row: As 2nd row.

7th row: As 3rd row to end, 14ch, turn, sl st into top of last tr of 3rd row, 2ch, 1dc into stem of previous tr, turn, 18tr into 14chsp, **do not turn.**

8th row: As 2nd row.

9th row: As 3rd row to end, then work over arch as follows: [2ch, miss 1tr, 1tr] 9 times, 2ch, sl st into 1st row, turn, *[2dc, 3ch, 2dc] into 2chsp; rep from * to end, **do not turn.**

Rows 10th to 12th rows: As 4th to 6th rows.

Rep from 3rd row 12 times more.

Next row: 5ch (count as 1tr, 2ch), miss first 3 sts 1tr into next st, *2ch, miss 2 sts, 1tr into next st; rep from * to end placing last tr into 3rd of 3ch, turn.

Edging: 1dc into first tr, *2dc into 2chsp, [1dc, 3ch, 1dc] into next tr; rep from * to end of row, then continue along top edge: **2dc into stem of tr, [1dc, 3ch, 1dc] into top of next st; rep from ** to end, then work along other side edge to match first side ending with 1dc into last st.

Fasten off.

BRIGHTER BATHROOMS

Bathrooms need never be entirely functional. A set of hand towels finished with these geometric edgings adds a decorative touch which is very easy to achieve. You don't have to make them in white, but could match the cotton you use to your colour scheme.

7
Diamond Edging
✪✪

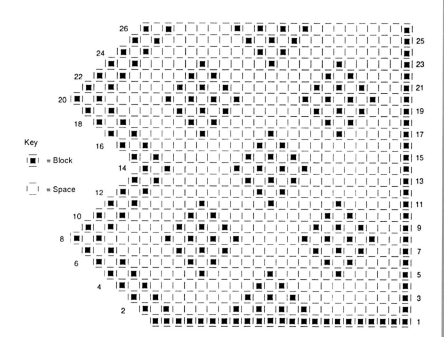

Key

$\boxed{\blacksquare}$ = Block

$\square$ = Space

Materials

Coats Patons Opera No. 20 Crochet Cotton Shade 500 - 100 grams

1.00mm Milward Steel Crochet Hook

To Make

Make 72ch.

1st row: 1tr into 4th ch from hook, 1tr into each ch to end, turn. 23 blks.

2nd row: Inc 1 blk, 1tr into first tr, 2ch, miss 2tr, 1tr into each of next 4tr (1 sp worked over 1 blk and 1 blk over 1 blk), [2ch, miss 2tr, 1tr into next tr] 5 times (5 sps worked over 5 blks), 1tr into each of next 3tr (1 blk worked over 1 blk), [2ch, miss 2tr, 1tr into each of next 4tr] 3 times, [2ch, miss 2tr, 1tr into next tr] 8 times, 1tr into each of next 2tr, 1tr into next ch (1 blk worked over 1 blk at end of row), turn.

3rd row: 3ch (count as 1tr), miss first tr, 1tr into each of next 3tr (1 blk worked over 1 blk at beg of row), [2ch, 1tr into next tr] 8 times, (8 sps worked over 8 sps), [2ch, miss 2tr, 1tr into next tr, 2tr into next sp, 1tr into next tr] 3 times, 2ch, miss 2tr, 1tr into next tr [2ch, 1tr into next tr], 5 times, 2ch, miss 2tr, 1tr into next tr, 2tr into next sp, 1tr into next tr, 2ch, miss 2tr, 1tr into last st, inc 1 blk, turn.

Continue following chart to end, then rep 15th to 26th rows inclusive as many times as required.

Final row: 3ch, miss first tr, work 1tr into each tr and 2tr into each sp to last blk. Do not fasten off and do not turn work.

Edging: Starting along sloped edge work as follows: *3ch, 1dc into corner of next blk; rep from * to 1st row inclusive, continue along side edge as follows: * 1dc into each of next 3 sts, 3ch; rep from * to end, then along top edge, work 2dc around stem of first st, 1dc into top of same st, *[1dc, 3ch, 1dc] around stem of next tr, 1dc into top of same tr; rep from * to end, then continue along side edge as before.

Work 1 more row along shaped edge: *work [2dc, 3ch, 2dc] into each 3ch sp to end, sl st into first dc of side edge.

8

Diamond Border

✪

Materials

Coats Patons Opera No. 20 Crochet Cotton Shade 500 - 100 grams

1.00mm Milward Steel Crochet Hook

To Make

Make 90ch.

1st row: 1tr into 4th ch from hook, 1tr into each ch to end, turn. (29 blks).

2nd row: 3ch (count as 1tr), miss first tr, 1tr into each of next 3tr, [2ch, miss 2tr, 1tr into next tr] 13 times, (13 sps over 13 blks), 1tr into each of next 3tr, (1 blk over 1 blk), 13 sps over 13 blks, 1tr into each of next 3 sts placing last tr into 3rd of 3ch.

3rd row: 3ch, miss first tr, 1tr into each of next 3tr, [2ch, 1tr into next tr] 12 times (12 sps over 12 sps), 2tr into next sp, 1tr into next tr, (1 blk over 1 sp), 2ch, miss 2tr, 1tr into each of next 3tr, (1 sp over 1blk, 1blk over 1 sp), 12 sps, 1 blk, turn.

Continue following chart to end then repeat 15th to 26th rows inclusive as many times as required.

Final row: 3ch, miss first tr, work 1 tr into each tr and 2tr into each sp to end, turn.

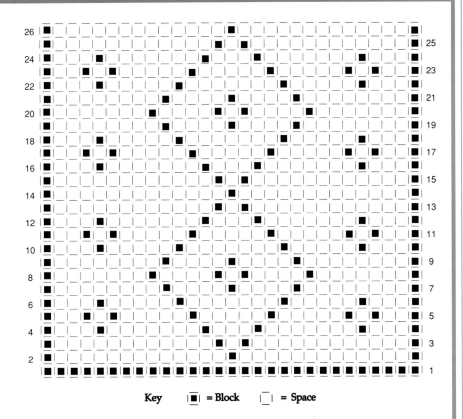

Key ▣ = Block ▢ = Space

Edging: 1ch, work 1dc into first tr, ★ *3ch, 1dc into each of next 3tr; rep from * to end of row, continue along long side as follows: 3ch, 2dc into first row, **[1dc, 3ch, 1dc] into next row, 2dc into next row; rep from ** to next corner, then rep from ★ once more, on remaining 2 sides, sl st into first dc.

Fasten off.

TIP

All crochet work regains its shine if ironed with a cotton cloth sprinkled with a little alcohol.

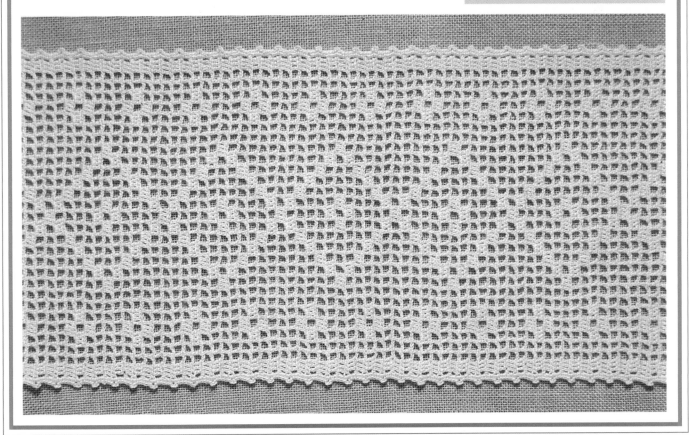

TEA TIME TREAT

Let this doily take centre stage at tea time.

9
Star Doily

⭐⭐

Materials

Coats Patons Musica No. 5 Crochet Cotton Shade 500 - 50 grams

1.75mm Milward Steel Crochet Hook

To Make

Make 10ch, join into a ring with a sl st.

1st round: Work 18dc in a ring, sl st into first dc.

2nd round: 6ch (count as 1tr, 3ch), miss first dc, *1tr into next dc, 3ch, miss next dc; rep from * to end, sl st into 3rd of 3ch.

3rd round: Sl st into first sp, 4ch (count as 1dtr), 2dtr into same sp, 3ch, *3dtr into next sp, 3ch; rep from * to end, sl st into 4th of 4ch.

4th round: 4ch, 1dtr into same st as last sl st, 1dtr into next dtr, 2dtr into next dtr, 3ch, *2dtr into next dtr, 1dtr into next dtr, 2dtr into next dtr, 3ch; rep from * to end, sl st into 4th of 4ch.

Working 1dtr into each dtr of previous round unless otherwise indicated continue as follows:

5th round: 4ch, 1dtr into same st as last sl st, 3dtr, 2dtr into next st, 3ch, *2dtr into next st, 3dtr, 2dtr into next st, 3ch; rep from * to end, sl st into 4th of 4ch.

6th round: 4ch, 1dtr into same st as last sl st, 5dtr, 2dtr into next st, 5ch, *2dtr into next st, 5dtr, 2dtr into next st, 5ch; rep from * to end, sl st into 4th of 4ch.

7th round: 4ch, 1dtr into same t as last sl st, 7dtr, 2dtr into next st, 5ch, *2dtr into next st, 7dtr, 2dtr into next st, 5ch; rep from * to end, sl st into 4th of 4ch.

8th round: Sl st into next dtr, 4ch, 8dtr, 5ch, 1dc into next sp, 5ch, miss 1dtr, * 9dtr, 5ch, 1dc into next sp, 5ch, miss 1dtr; rep from * to end, sl st into 4th of 4ch.

9th round: Sl st into next dtr, 4ch, 6dtr, 5ch, miss 4ch, 1htr into each of next 3 sts, 5ch, miss 1dtr, *7dtr, 5ch, miss 4ch,

1htr into each of next 3 sts, 5ch, miss 1dtr; rep from * to end, sl st into 4th of 4ch.

10th round: Sl st into next dtr, 4ch, 4dtr, 6ch, miss 4ch, 1htr into each of next 5 sts, 6ch, miss 1dtr, * 5dtr, 6ch, miss 4ch, 1htr into each of next 5 sts, 6ch, miss 1dtr; rep from * to end, sl st into 4th of 4ch.

11th round: Sl st into next dtr, 4ch, 2dtr, 7ch, miss 5ch, 7htr, 7ch, miss 1dtr, * 3dtr, 7ch, miss 5ch, 7htr, 7ch, miss 1dtr; rep from * to end, sl st into 4th of 4ch.

12th round: 4ch, 2dtr, 9ch, miss 1htr, 5htr, 9ch, *3dtr, 9ch, miss 1htr, 5htr, 9ch; rep from * to end, sl st into 4th of 4ch.

13th round: 4ch, *[1dtr, 5ch, 1dtr] into next st, 1dtr, 1dtr into next ch, 10ch, miss 1htr, 3htr, 10ch, miss 8ch, 2dtr; rep from * to end omitting 1dtr at end of last rep, sl st into 4th of 4ch.

14th round: 4ch, *1dtr, 7ch, 1dc into next sp, 7ch, 3dtr, 9ch, miss 1htr, 1htr, 9ch, 2dtr, rep from * to end omitting 1dtr at end of last rep, sl st into 4th of 4ch.

15th round: 4ch, *1dtr, [7ch, 1dc into next sp] twice, 7ch, 3dtr, 9ch, 1dtr into each of next 2dtr; rep from * to end omitting 1dtr at end of last rep, sl st into 4th of 4ch.

16th round: 4ch, *1dtr, 7ch, 1dc into next sp, 12dtr into next sp, 1dc into next sp, 7ch, 2dtr, sl st into 9chsp, miss 1dtr, 1dtr; rep from * to end omitting 1tr at end of last rep, sl st into 4th of 4ch.

17th round: *2sl st, 8dc into next 7chsp, [4dc, 1 picot (see Special Abbreviations on page 5)] 3 times, 2dc, 8dc into next sp, 3sl st*; rep from * to end.

Fasten off.

10

Pine Cone Doily

✪✪

Materials

Coats Patons Musica No. 5 Crochet Cotton Shade 500 - 50 grams

1.75mm Milward Steel Crochet Hook

To Make

Make 12ch, join into a ring with a sl st.

1st round: 3ch (count as 1tr), work 23tr into ring, sl st into 3rd of 3ch.

2nd round: 6ch (count as 1tr, 3ch), miss next tr, [1tr into next tr, 3ch, miss 1tr] 11 times, sl st into 3rd of 6ch.

3rd round: 3ch (count as 1tr), *4tr into next sp, 1tr into next tr; rep from * to end omitting 1tr, at end of last rep, sl st into 3rd of 3ch. 60tr.

4th round: 3ch, 1tr into each tr to end, sl st into 3rd of 3ch.

5th round: 3ch (count as 1tr), 1tr into next tr, tr2tog over next 2tr, 1tr into each of next 2tr, 2ch, [1tr into each of next 2tr, tr2tog over next 2tr, 1tr into each of next 2tr, 2ch] 7 times, sl st into 3rd of 3ch.

6th round: 3ch, 1tr into next tr, tr2tog over next 2 sts, 1tr into next tr, 2ch, 1tr into 2ch arch, 2ch, [1tr into each of next 2tr, tr2tog over 2 sts, 1tr into next tr, 2ch, 1tr into next 2ch arch, 2ch] 7 times, sl st into 3rd of 3ch.

Working 1tr into each tr unless otherwise indicated, continue as follows:

7th round: 3ch, tr3tog over next 3tr, [3ch, 1tr into next arch] twice, 3ch, *tr4tog over next 4tr, [3ch, 1tr into next arch] twice, 3ch; rep from * to end, sl st into top of tr3tog.

8th round: Sl st into centre of first arch, 6ch (count as 1tr 3ch), *1tr into next arch, 3ch; rep from * to end, sl st into 3rd of 6ch.

9th round: Sl st into centre of first arch, 6ch, 1tr into next arch, 3ch, [3tr, 2ch, 3tr, 3ch] into next arch, *[1tr into next arch, 3ch] twice, [3tr, 2ch, 3tr, 3ch] into next arch; rep from * to end, sl st into 3rd of 6ch.

10th round: Sl st into first arch, 3ch, 2tr into same arch as last sl st, 1ch, 3tr into next arch, 1ch, 3tr, 2ch, 3tr, 1ch, [3tr into next arch, 1ch] 3 times, *3tr, 2ch, 3tr, 1ch, [3tr into next arch, 1ch] 3 times; rep from * 6 times more omitting 3tr and 1ch at end of last rep, sl st, into 3rd of 3ch.

11th round: Sl st into next 2tr and ch, 5ch (count as 1tr, 2ch), miss 3tr, 3tr, 2ch, 3tr, 2ch, miss 1 sp, 1tr into next sp, 3ch, *1tr into next sp, 2ch, miss 3tr, 3tr, 2ch, 3tr, 2ch, miss 1sp, 1tr into next sp, 3ch; rep from * to end, sl st into 3rd of 5ch.

12th round: Sl st into next tr, 3ch (count as 1tr), 1tr into each of next 2tr, 2ch, 3tr, 2ch, miss 1sp, 5tr into next sp, 2ch, *3tr, 2ch, 3tr, 2ch, miss 1sp, 5tr into next sp, 2ch; rep from * to end, sl st into 3rd of 3ch.

Working first tr as 3ch, continue as follows:

13th round: *3tr, 2ch, 3tr, 2ch, [1tr 1ch into next st] 4 times, 1tr, 2ch; rep from * to end, sl st into first tr.

14th round: 3ch, *3tr, 2tr into next sp, 3tr, 2ch, [1dc into next 1chsp, 3ch] 3 times, 1dc into 1chsp, 2ch; rep from * to end, sl st into first tr.

15th round: *2tr, 1ch, 2tr, 3ch, 2tr, 1ch, 2tr, 2ch, [1dc into 3ch arch, 3ch] twice, 1dc into next 3ch arch, 2ch; rep from * to end, sl st into first tr.

16th round: *2tr, 1ch, 2tr, 2ch, [1tr, 1ch] 4 times into next 3ch arch, 1tr into same arch, 2ch, 2tr, 1ch, 2tr, 2ch, 1dc into 3ch arch, 3ch, 1dc, into next 3ch arch, 2ch; rep from * to end, sl st into first tr.

17th round: *2tr, 1ch, 2tr, 2ch [1dc into next chsp, 3ch] 3 times, 1dc into next chsp, 2ch, 2tr, 1ch, 2tr, 2ch, 1dc into 3ch arch, 2ch; rep from * to end, sl st into first tr.

18th round: *2tr, 1ch, 2tr, [3ch, 1dc into next 3ch arch] 3 times, 3ch, 2tr, 1ch, 2tr, 3ch; rep from * to end, sl st into first tr.

19th round: *2tr, 1ch, 2tr, 4ch, miss 1 arch, 1dc into next arch, 3ch, 1dc into next arch, 4ch, 2tr, 1ch, 2tr, 2ch, [1tr, 2ch] 4 times into next 3ch arch; rep from * to end, sl st into first tr.

20th round: *2tr, 1ch, 2tr, 4ch, miss 1 arch, 1dc into next 3ch arch, 4ch, 2tr, 1ch, 2tr, [2ch, 1tr into next 2chsp] twice, 2ch, 3tr into next sp, 2ch [1tr into next sp, 2ch] twice; rep from * to end, sl st into first tr.

21st round: *2tr, 1ch, 2tr, 2ch, miss next 2 arches, 2tr, 1ch, 2tr, [2ch, 1tr into next 2chsp] 3 times, 2ch, miss 1tr, 1tr into next tr, 2ch, [1tr into next 2chsp, 2ch] 3 times; rep from * to end, sl st into first tr.

22nd round: *[2tr, 1ch] twice, 2tr into next sp, [1ch, 2tr] twice, [3ch, 1tr into next sp] 8 times, 3ch; rep from * to end, sl st into first tr.

Fasten off.

11
Fan Doily

✪✪

Materials

Coats Patons Musica No. 5 Crochet Cotton Shade 500 - 50 grams.
1.75mm Milward Steel Crochet Hook

To Make

Make 12ch, join into a ring with a sl st.

1st round: 3ch (count as 1tr), work 23tr into ring, sl st into 3rd of 3ch.

2nd round: 3ch, 1tr into each of next 2tr, 4ch, [1tr into each of next 3tr, 4ch] 7 times, sl st into 3rd of 3ch.

3rd round: Sl st to first sp, [3ch (count as 1tr), 2tr, 3ch, 3tr] into same sp as last sl st, 3ch, *[3tr, 3ch, 3tr] into next 4ch sp, 3ch; rep from * to end, sl st into 3rd of 3ch. 8 groups of fans.

4th round: Sl st to first sp, [3ch, 2tr, 3ch, 3tr] into same sp as last sl st, 4ch, *[3tr, 3ch, 3tr] into next 3chsp, 4ch; rep from * to end, sl st into 3rd of 3ch.

5th round: Sl st to first sp, [3ch, 2tr, 3ch, 3tr] into same sp as last sl st, 6ch, *[3tr, 3ch, 3tr] into next 3chsp, 6ch; rep from * to end, sl st into 3rd of 3ch.

6th round: Sl st to first sp, 1dc into same sp as last sl st, *7ch, 1dtr between 2 groups of fans formed on 3rd round (at the same time catch arches formed on previous 2 rounds), 7ch, 1dc into next 3ch sp; rep from * to end omitting 1dc at end of last rep, sl st into first dc.

7th round: 3ch, *7tr into next arch, 1tr into next dtr, 7tr into next arch, 1tr into next dc; rep from * to end omitting 1tr at end of last rep, sl st into 3rd of 3ch. 128tr.

8th round: 3ch, 1tr into next tr, 6ch, miss 5tr, *1tr into each of next 3tr, 6ch, miss 5tr; rep from * to end, sl st into 3rd of 3ch.

9th round: Sl st to first arch, [3ch, 2tr, 3ch, 3tr] into same arch as last sl st, 3ch, *[3tr, 3ch, 3tr] into next arch, 3ch; rep from * to end, sl st into 3rd of 3ch. 16 groups of fans.

10th to 15th rounds: Rep to 9th rounds (16 groups of fans on 10th round and 32 groups on 15th round).

16th and 17th round: As 4th and 5th rounds

18th round: Sl st to first sp, 5ch (count as 1dtr, 1ch), [1dtr, 1ch] 6 times and 1dtr into same sp as last sl st, 1dtr between 2 groups of fans formed 3 rows below (as 6th round), *[1dtr, 1ch] 7 times and 1dtr into next 3chsp, 1dtr between 2 groups of fans as before; rep from * to end, sl st into 4th of 5ch.

19th round: Sl st to first chsp, 1dc into same sp as sl st, *4ch, 1dc into next chsp; rep from * to end omitting 1dc at end of last rep, sl st into first dc.
Fasten off.

COOL ELEGANCE

10

Two versatile doilies for any occasion - ideal for lining a toiletry basket or just for show on your dining table.

12
Floral Edging
★★★

Materials

Coats Patons Opera No. 20 Crochet Cotton Shade 500 - 50 grams.
1.00mm Milward Steel Crochet Hook

Top Row of Flowers

★ First Flower

Make 4ch, join into a ring with a sl st.

1st round: Work 8dc into the ring, sl st into first dc.

2nd round: 1dc into back loop only of same st as last sl st, *8ch, 1dc into 2nd ch from hook, working 1st into every ch, 1htr, 4tr, 1ch, sl st into back loop only of same st of 1st round as last dc, 1dc into back loop only of next dc; rep from * to end omitting dc at end of last rep.

3rd round: Sl st to base of tr nearest tip of first petal, 3ch (count as 1tr), *3ch, 1dc into tip of petal, 3ch, 1tr into first tr of same petal, 1tr into base of tr nearest tip of next petal; rep from * to end omitting 1tr at end of last rep, sl st into 3rd of 3ch at beg of round.

4th round: Working first dtr of first dtr3tog as a 4ch *[dtr3tog, 1 picot (see Special Abbreviations on page 5), 3ch, dtr3tog, 1 picot] into sp formed by the 3tr between tip of 2 bars, 3ch, [1dc, 3ch, 1dc] into next dc; rep from * to end, sl st into top of first dtr3tog. 8 double petals. Fasten off.

Second Flower

Work the first 3 rounds as given for First Flower, then join as follows:

4th round: Work as 4th round but replace the first picot of first double flower by ajoining picot into first picot of a double petal on first flower, and the 2nd picot of same double flower by ajoining picot into 2nd picot of same petal on first flower, complete round as for first flower.

Work 8 more flowers in the same way joining them into a strip as before, thus leaving 3 double petals free at top and bottom ★.

Top Edging

With right side facing rejoin yarn to first picot of 3rd petal to the right of join with 2nd flower.

1st row: 9 ch (count as 1dtr, 5ch), *1ttr into 2nd picot of same petal, [5ch, 1dc into next picot] twice, 5ch, 1tr into next picot, 5ch, ttr2tog working first st into

next picot and 2nd st into corresponding picot of next flower, 5ch; rep from * to end but working 1dtr in place of ttr2tog at end of last rep, and omitting 5ch, turn.

2nd row: 5ch (count as 1tr, 2ch), miss first 3 sts, *1tr into next st, 2ch, miss 2 sts; rep from * to end, 1tr into 4th of 9ch, turn.

3rd row: sl st into first sp, *[2dc, 3ch, 2dc] into each sp to end. Fasten off.

Lower Arches

With right side facing, rejoin yarn to first picot of 2nd free double petal of first flower and work first row as for Top Edging. Fasten off.

Second Row of Flowers

Work as given for First Row from ★ to ★.

Joining Row of Arches

Work as first row of Top Edging but joining each arch to corresponding arch of top row by working [2ch, sl st into corresponding arch of top row, 2ch] throughout.

Third Row

First Flower

Work first 3 rounds as given for First Flower of Top Row, then join to first and 2nd flowers of 2nd row as follows:

4th round: Work as 4th round of First Flower, but joining to first and 2nd flowers of 2nd row as follows: replace 2nd picot of first double petal by a joining picot into 2nd picot of 3rd free double petal of first flower, in the same way join next 2 picots to next 2 picots of first flower, next 2 picots to corresponding free petal of 2nd flower, then next picot to next picot of 2nd flower, complete 4th round as for first flower.

Work 4 more flowers in the same way, joining each one to next pair of flowers.

Lower Edging and Filling Arches

With wrong side facing rejoin yarn with a dc into arch of first free petal of first flower on 2nd row, 12ch, 1 tr into arch of next petal, *12ch, ttr2tog working into next picot of same flower and first free picot of next flower, working around flower at point continue as follows: [12ch, 1tr into next free arch of petal] twice, 6ch, 1dtr into 3ch arch between the 2dc, 6ch, 1tr into arch of next petal, 12ch, 1tr into arch of next petal, 12 ch, ttr2tog working into next picot and first free picot of next flower, 12ch, 1tr into arch of next petal, 8ch,

1tr into arch of first free petal of next flower; rep from * to end omitting 8ch at end of last rep, work 12ch, 1dc into next free arch of last petal, turn.

Working into previous arches and forming arches between flowers, continue as follows:

Work 15dc into each of first 4 arches, 10dc into next arch, *3ch, 10dc into next arch, 15dc into each of next 3 arches, [4dc, 3ch, 4dc] into next arch between 2 flowers on 2nd row, 8dc into next arch, turn, 12ch, sl st into 3rd dc on arch between the 2 flowers, turn, 9dc into arch just formed, 12ch, turn, sl st into 6th dc of same arch as last sl st, turn, 9dc into arch just formed, 4ch, turn, sl st into 8th dc of previous 15dc arch, turn, work joining horizontal arches consisting of [3dc, 3ch, 3dc] into each of next 3 arches, 7dc into same 15ch arch as last 8dc, 8dc into next arch, 13ch, turn, sl st into 5th dc of joining arch, 10dc into arch just formed, [13ch, turn, miss 2dc on joining arch, sl st into next dc, turn, 10dc into arch just formed] 3 times, 5ch, turn, sl st into 8th dc of next 15dc arch, turn, work 2nd row of joining horizontal arches consisting of [4dc, 3ch, 4dc] into each of next 5 arches, 7dc into same arch as last 8dc, 8dc into next arch, 15ch, turn, sl st into 8th dc of next joining horizontal arch, turn, 10dc into arch just formed, [15ch, turn, miss 7dc of horizontal arches, sl st into next dc, turn, 10dc into arch just formed] 3 times, 5ch, turn, sl st into 8th dc on next 15dc arch, work 3rd row of joining horizontal arches consisting of [5dc, 3ch, 5dc] into each of next 5 arches, 7dc into same arch as last 8dc, 5dc into next 6ch arch, turn, [12ch, 1dc into 10th dc of next horizontal arch] 4 times, 12ch, sl st into 5th of 10dc arch, turn, work final row of horinzontal arches consisting of [8dc, 3ch, 8dc] into each of next 5 arches, 5dc into same 6ch arch as last 5dc; rep from * 3 times, 3ch, 10dc into next 6ch arch, 15dc into each of last 4 arches. Fasten off.

13
Scalloped Border
✪✪

Materials

Coats Patons Opera No. 20 Crochet Cotton Shade 500 - 50 grams.
1.00mm Milward Steel Crochet Hook

To Make

Make 236 ch.

1st row: 1dc into 2nd ch from hook, 1dc into each ch to end. 235dc.

2nd to 10th rows inclusive: 1ch, 1dc into each st to end.

Work the five scallops separately over 47sts as follows.

11th row: 1ch, dc2tog, dc to last 2 sts, dc2tog.

12th to 14th rows: As 11th row. 41dc remain

15th row: 1ch, dc2tog, 1dc into each of next 18dc, work popcorn as follows: 8dtr around centre dc **5 rows below**, drop loop from hook, insert hook from front to back into top of first of these dtr, pick up dropped loop and draw through dtr, secure popcorn by working 1dc into next st (centre st) on previous row, 1dc into each of next 18dc, dc2tog, turn.

16th to 18th rows: As 11th row.

Fasten off.

Work remaining 4 scallops in same way.

Lower Edging

With right side facing, rejoin yarn to side edge of 11th row on first scallop and work as follows:

1st row: Work 57dc evenly around each of the 5 scallops, ending at 11th row of side edge on last scallop. 290dc.

2nd row: 5ch (count as 1tr, 2ch), miss 2dc, **[1dc into next dc, 5ch, miss 3dc] 5 times, [1dc into next dc, 5ch, miss 2dc] 6 times, [1dc into next dc, 5ch, miss 3dc] 4 times*, sl st into first dc on next scallop, turn, 3dc into 5chsp just made, turn, 2ch, miss 2dc on next scallop; rep from ** 3 times more, then rep from ** to * once more omitting 5ch at end of rep, 2ch, 1tr into last dc, turn.

3rd row: 1ch, 1dc into first tr, 2dc into 2chsp, ** 6dc into each of next 14 5chsp, 2dc into next 2chsp*, 2dc into same sp as the 3dc of previous row; rep from ** 3 times more, then rep from ** to * once, 1dc into 3rd of 5ch, turn.

4th row: 5ch, **[1dc into 3rd dc of next arch, 5ch] 14 times*, sl st into 2nd st of

Here is another set of trimmings for your bathroom, one delicate, the other simpler and stronger. Again, don't limit yourself to our colour choice, but feel free to choose your own.

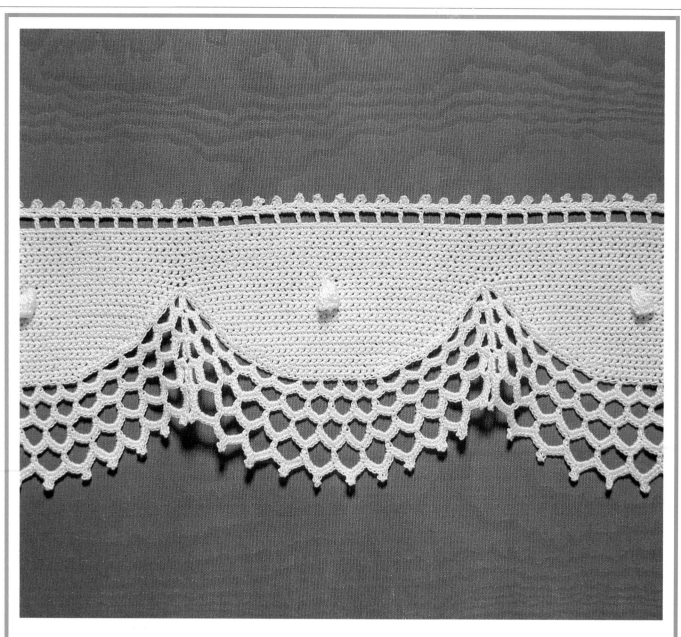

next arch, turn, 3dc into last 5chsp made, turn, 2ch, rep from ** 3 times, then rep from ** to * again, 2ch, 1tr into last dc.

5th row: 1ch, 1dc into first tr, 2dc into 2chsp, **[6dc into next chsp] 14 times, 2dc in 2chsp*, 2dc into same sp as 3dc of 4th row; rep from ** 3 times more, then rep from ** to * again, 1dc into 3rd of 5ch.

6th row: 5ch, **[1dc into 3rd st of next loop, 5ch] 13 times*, sl st into 2nd st of next loop, turn, 3dc into last 5chsp made, turn, 2ch; rep from ** 3 times more then rep from ** to * again omitting 5ch at end of last rep, 2ch, 1tr into last dc.

7th row: 1ch, 1dc into first tr, 2dc into 2chsp, **[6dc into next chsp] 13 times*, 2dc into 2chsp, 2dc into same sp as 3dc of 6th row; rep from ** 3 times more, then rep from ** to * again, 1dc into 3rd of 5ch.

8th row: 5ch, **[1dc into 3rd st of next loop, 7ch] 11 times*, 1dc into next sp, 5ch, sl st into 2nd st of next loop, turn,

3dc into last 5chsp made, turn, 2ch; rep from ** 3 times more, then rep from ** to * again, 2ch, 1tr into last st, turn.

9th row: 1ch, 1dc into first tr, 2dc into 2chsp, **[4dc 1 picot (see Special Abbreviations on page 5) 4dc into next loop] 11 times*, 1dc into 2chsp, 1dc into same sp as 3dc of 8th row; rep from ** 3 times more, then rep from ** to * again, 1dc into 3rd of 5ch.

Side and Top Edge

Continuing along side edge arches work as follows: 1 picot, 5dc into same loop as 2dc just worked, [1 picot, 4dc into next loop] 3 times, along straight edge work 2dc, [1 picot, 5dc] twice, 1 picot. Continue along starting ch with 5ch, *miss 2 sts, 1tr, 2ch; rep from * to end. Along other side edge work [1 picot, 5dc] twice, 1 picot, 2dc, in each arch work 4dc, 1 picot, Fasten off.

With right side facing rejoin yarn to first st of top edge and work *1 picot, 3dc into 2chsp; rep from * to end, 1 picot. Fasten off.

14

Lacy Doily

✪✪

Materials

Coats Patons Opera No. 20 Crochet Cotton Shade 500 - 50 grams

1.00mm Milward Steel Crochet Hook

To Make

1st round: Make 4ch, and work 11tr into first of these ch, sl st into 3rd of 3ch.

2nd round: 6ch (count as 1tr, 3ch), [1tr into next tr, 3ch] 11 times, sl st into 3rd of 6ch.

3rd round: 7ch (count as 1tr, 4ch), [1tr into next tr, 4ch] 11 times, sl st into 3rd of 7ch.

4th round: 9ch (count as 1tr, 6ch), [1tr into next tr, 6ch] 11 times, sl st into 3rd of 9ch.

5th round: Sl st into first sp, work [1dc, 3ch, 5tr, 3ch, 1dc] into each of the 12sps, sl st into first dc.

6th round: Sl st into first 4sts, 3ch (count as 1tr) 1tr into each of next 4tr, 5ch [1tr into each of next 5tr, 5ch] 11 times, sl st into 3rd of 3ch.

7th round: 3ch, tr2tog over next 2tr, (tr3tog at beg of round), 5ch, 1dc into 3rd of 5ch arch, 5ch, miss 1tr, *tr3tog over next 3 sts, 5ch, 1dc into 3rd of 5ch arch, 5ch, miss 1tr; rep from * to end, sl st into 3rd of 3ch.

8th round: *1dc into next tr3tog, 5ch, 3tr into next dc, 5ch; rep from * to end, sl st into first dc.

9th round: Sl st into next 6 sts, 3ch (count as 1tr), 1tr into same st as last sl st, 1tr into next tr, 2tr into next tr, 10ch, *2tr into next tr, 1tr into next tr, 2tr into next tr; rep from * to end, sl st into 3rd of 3ch.

10th round: 3ch, 1tr into same st as last sl st, *1tr into each of next 3tr, 2tr into next tr, 6ch, 1dc into sp, 6ch, 2tr into next tr; rep from * to end omitting 2tr at end of last rep, sl st into 3rd of 3ch.

11th round: 10ch (count as 1tr, 7ch), miss 5tr, 1tr into next tr, 7ch, *1tr into next tr, 7ch, miss 5tr, 1tr into next tr, 7ch; rep from * to end, sl st into 3rd of 10ch.

12th round: Sl st into first sp, work [1dc, 3ch, 7tr, 3ch, 1dc] into each sp to end, sl st into first dc.

13th round: Sl st to 2nd tr, 3ch, 1tr into each of next 4tr, 9ch, miss 1tr, *1tr into each of next 5tr, 9ch, miss 1tr; rep from * to end, sl st into 3rd of 3ch.

Work 7th to 13th round inclusive once more.

21st round: Sl st into next st, 3ch, tr2tog over next 2 sts, 4ch, 1dc into next sp, 4ch, miss 1tr, *tr3tog over next 3 sts, 4ch, 1dc into next sp, 4ch, miss 1tr; rep from * to end, sl st into 3rd of 13ch.

22nd round: 13ch, (count as 1tr, 10ch) *1tr into top of next tr3tog, 10ch; rep from * to end, sl st into 3rd of 13ch.

23rd round: 1dc into same st as last sl st, 5ch, 1dc into next sp, 5ch, *1dc into next tr, 5ch, 1dc into next sp, 5ch; rep from * to end, sl st into first dc.

24th round: Sl st to centre of first arch, *1dc into arch, 5ch; rep from * to end, sl st into first dc.

25th round: Sl st to centre of first arch, *1dc into arch, 6ch; rep from * to end, sl st into first dc.

26th round: Sl st to centre of first arch, *1dc into arch, 7ch; rep from * to end, sl st into first dc.

27th round: Sl st to centre of first arch, 9ch, *1tr into 4th of 7chsp, 6ch; rep from * to end, sl st into 3rd of 9ch.

28th round: Sl st into first arch, 3ch, 5tr into same arch, 6tr into next arch, 3ch, 1dc into next arch, 3ch, *[6tr into next arch] twice, 3ch, 1dc into next arch, 3ch; rep from * to end, sl st into 3rd of 3ch.

29th round: Sl st into next tr, 3ch, 1tr into each of next 9tr, miss 1tr, *1tr, 9ch, miss 1tr, *1tr into each of next 10tr, 9ch, miss 1tr; rep from * to end, sl st into 3rd of 3ch.

30th round: Sl st into each of next 2tr, 3ch, 1tr into each of next 5tr, 6ch, 1dc into next arch, 6ch, miss 2tr, *1tr into each of next 6tr, 6ch, 1dc, into next arch, 6ch, miss 2tr; rep from * to end, sl st into 3rd of 3ch.

31st round: Sl st into each of next 3tr, 6ch (count as 1tr, 3ch), 1tr into same st as last sl st, 9ch, 1dc into next dc, 9ch, *miss 3tr, [1tr, 3ch, 1tr] between 3rd and 4th tr of next 6tr group, 9ch, 1dc into next dc, 9ch; rep from * to end, sl st into 3rd of 6ch.

32nd round: 5ch (count as 1tr, 2ch), [1tr, 2ch, 1tr] into next 3ch arch, 2ch, 1tr into next tr, 7ch, 1dc into next dc, 7ch, *1tr into next tr, 2ch, [1tr, 2ch, 1tr] into next arch, 2ch, 1tr into next tr, 7ch, 1dc into next dc, 7ch; rep from * to end, sl st into 3rd of 5ch.

33rd round: 3ch, 2tr in first sp, 1tr into next tr, [1tr, 1 picot (see Special Abbreviations on page 5) 1tr] into next sp, 1tr into next tr, 2tr into next sp, 1tr into next tr, 5tr into next 7ch arch, tr2tog placing first tr into same arch as last 5tr and next into next 7ch arch, 5tr into same arch as last tr, *1tr into next tr, 2tr into next sp, 1tr into next tr, [1tr, 1 picot, 1tr] into next sp, 1tr into next tr, 2tr into next sp, 1tr into next tr, 5tr into next arch, tr2tog as before, 5tr into same arch, sl st into 3rd of 3ch. Fasten off.

ROMANTIC ROSE

Sometimes nothing but the best will do, and that's where these doilies come into their own. For special occasions they lend an elegant air to whatever you are serving.

15
Small Doily

✪✪

Materials

Coats Patons Opera No. 20 Crochet Cotton Shade 500 - 50 grams

1.00mm Milward Steel Crochet Hook

To Make

Make 4 ch, join into a ring with a sl st.

1st round: 12dc into ring, sl st into first dc.

2nd round: 7ch (count as 1tr, 4ch), *miss 1 st, 1tr into next dc, 4ch; rep from * to end, sl st into 3rd of 7ch.

3rd round: Sl st into first sp, 3ch (count as 1tr), 4tr into same sp, 4ch, *5tr into next sp, 4ch; rep from * to end, sl st into 3rd of 7ch.

4th round: 3ch (count as 1tr), miss next 3tr, 1tr into next tr until 2 loops remain on hook, yo and through the 2 loops (tr2tog at beg of round), 5ch, 1tr into same tr as 2nd tr of previous tr2tog until 2 loops remain on hook, 1tr into next tr until 3 loops remain on hook, yo and through the 3 loops, 5ch, *1tr into 2nd tr of previous tr2tog, miss 3tr, 1tr into next tr until 3 loops remain, yo and through the 3 loops, 5ch, 1tr into same tr as 2nd tr of previous tr2tog until 2 loops remain on hook, 1tr into next tr until 3 loops remain on hook, yo and through the 3 loops, 5ch; rep from * to end placing 2nd tr of last tr2tog into 3rd of 3ch at beg of previous round, sl st into first tr2tog.

5th round: 7ch, (count as 1dtr, 3ch), 1dtr into same st as last sl st, 3ch, 1tr into next sp, 3ch, 1dc into tr2tog, 3ch, 1tr into next sp, 3ch, [1dtr, 3ch, 1dtr] into tr2tog, 3ch, 1tr into next sp, 3ch, 1dc into tr2tog, 3ch, 1tr into next sp, 3ch; rep from * to end, sl st into 3rd of 7ch.

6th round: Sl st into first sp, 9ch, 1ttr into dc, 9ch, miss 2sp, 1dc into next sp, 9ch; rep from * to end, sl st into first dc.

7th round: Sl st into next sp, *[1dc, 4ch] 5 times into 9chsp; rep from * to end, 4ch, sl st into first dc.

8th round: Sl st to centre of next sp, *9ch, miss 2 sp, 1dc into next sp, 9ch, miss 1 sp, 1dc into next sp; rep from * to end, sl st into first dc.

9th round: Sl st to centre of first sp, 3ch, [1tr, 2ch, 2tr] into same sp, [5ch, 1tr] twice into next sp, 5ch, [2tr, 2ch, 2tr] into next sp, [5ch, 1tr] twice in next sp, 5ch; rep from * to end, sl st into 3rd of 3ch.

10th round: 3ch (count as 1tr), 1tr into

next tr, 2ch, 1tr into each of next 2tr, 6ch, miss 1sp, 1dc into next sp, 6ch, *1tr into each of next 2tr, 2ch, 1tr into each of next 2tr, 6ch, miss 1 sp, 1dc into next sp, 6ch; rep from * to end, sl st into 3rd of 3ch.

Counting 3ch at beginning of each round as 1tr and working 1tr into each tr, unless otherwise indicated, continue as follows:

11th round: 3ch, [1tr, 2ch, 2tr, 5ch, 1dc] into next sp, 7ch, 1dc into next sp, 5ch, *[2tr, 2ch, 2tr, 5ch, 1dc] into next sp, 7ch, 1dc into next sp, 5ch; rep from * to end, sl st into 3rd of 3ch.

12th round: 3ch, 1tr, 2ch, 2tr, 7ch, miss 5chsp, [1tr, 3ch, 1tr] in next sp, 7ch, *2tr, 2ch, 2tr, 7ch, miss 5chsp, [1tr, 3ch, 1tr] into next sp, 7ch; rep from * to end, sl st into 3rd of 3ch.

13th round: 3ch, [1tr, 2ch, 2tr, 5ch, 1dc] into 7chsp, 5ch, [1dc, 7ch, 1dc] into next sp, 5ch, 1dc into 7chsp, 5ch, *[2tr, 2ch, 2tr, 5ch, 1dc] into 7chsp, 5ch, [1dc, 7ch, 1dc] into next sp, 5ch, 1dc into 7chsp, 5ch; rep from * to end, sl st into 3rd of 3ch.

14th round: 3ch, 1tr, 2ch, 2tr, 5ch, [1dtr, 2ch] 7 times and 1dtr into 7chsp, 5ch, *2tr, 2ch, 2tr, 5ch, [1dtr, 2ch] 7 times and 1dtr into 7chsp, 5ch;

rep from * to end, sl st into 3rd of 3ch.

15th round: 3ch, tr3tog over next 3tr, 5ch, [tr3tog into 2chsp, 5ch] 7 times, *tr4tog over next 4tr, 5ch, [tr3tog into 2chsp, 5ch] 7 times; rep from * to end, sl st into top of first tr3tog.

16th round: Sl st to centre of first sp, 1dc into same sp, *[2dc, 1 picot (see Special Abbreviations on page 5), 2dc into next 5chsp] 6 times, 1dc into next sp, 1 picot, 1dc into next sp; rep from * to end omitting 1dc at end of last rep, sl st into first dc. Fasten off.

TIP

Fresh stains of tea or coffee on cotton fabrics should be washed in soap and water, and bleached if possible.

If the stains have been there for a while try and soften the fabric with glycerine before removing stains.

16
Windmill Doily

✪✪

Materials

Coats Patons Opera No. 20 Crochet Cotton Shade 500 - 50 grams.

1.00mm Milward Steel Crochet Hook

To Make

Make 8ch, join into a ring with a sl st.

1st round: 3ch (count as 1tr), work 15tr into ring, sl st into 3rd of 3ch.

2nd round: 3ch, 1tr into same st as last sl st, *2tr into next st; rep from * to end, sl st into 3rd of 3ch. 32 sts.

3rd round: 1ch, 1dc into first st, 5ch, miss 3 sts, *1dc into next st, 5ch, miss 3 sts; rep from * to end, sl st into first dc.

4th round: Sl st into first sp, 3ch, into same sp work [1tr, 1ch, 1tr], 4ch, *[2tr, 1ch, 1tr] into next sp, 4ch; rep from * to end, sl st into 3rd of 3ch.

5th round: Sl st into next tr, 3ch, 2tr into chsp, 1ch, 1tr into next tr, 4ch, *miss 1tr, 1tr into next tr, 2tr into chsp, 1tr into next tr, 4ch; rep from * to end, sl st into 3rd of 3ch.

6th round: Sl st into next tr, 3ch, 1tr into next tr, 2tr into chsp, 1tr into next tr, 5ch, *miss 1tr, 1tr into each of next 2tr, 2tr into chsp, 1tr into next tr, 5ch; rep from * to end, sl st into 3rd of 3ch.

7th round: Sl st into next tr, 3ch, 1tr into next tr, 2tr into next tr, 2tr into chsp, 1ch, 1tr into next tr, 5ch, *miss 1tr, 1tr into each of next 2tr, 2tr into chsp, 1ch, 1tr into next tr, 5ch; rep from * to end, sl st into 3rd of 3ch

Replace first tr of round with 3ch and working 1tr into each tr, unless otherwise indicated continue as follows:

8th round: Sl st into next tr, *4tr, 2tr in next st, 2tr into sp, 1ch, 1tr, 5ch, miss 1 st; rep from * to end, sl st into first tr.

9th round: Sl st into next tr, *6tr, 2tr into next st, 2tr into sp, 1ch, 1tr, 5ch, miss st; rep from * to end, sl st into first tr.

10th round: Sl st into next tr, *8tr, 2tr into next st, 2tr into sp, 1ch, 1tr, 5ch, miss 1 st; rep from * to end, sl st into first tr.

11th round: Sl st into next tr, *10tr, 2tr into next st, 2tr into sp, 1ch, 1tr, 5ch, miss 1 st, rep from * to end, sl st into first tr.

12th round: Sl st into next tr, *12tr, 2tr into next st, 2tr into sp, 1ch, 1tr, 5ch, miss 1 st; rep from * to end, sl st into first tr.

13th round: Sl st into next tr, *14tr, 2tr into next st, 2tr into sp, 1ch, 1tr, 5ch, miss 1 st, rep from * to end, sl st into first dc.

14th round: Sl st into next tr, *16tr, 2tr in next st, 2tr into sp, 1ch, 1tr, 5ch, miss 1 st; rep from * to end, sl st into first tr.

15th round: Sl st into next tr, *18tr, 2tr in next st, 2tr into sp, 1ch, 1tr, 5ch, miss 1 st, rep from * to end, sl st into first tr.

16th round: Sl st into next tr, *20tr, 2tr in next st, 2tr into sp, 1ch, 1tr, 5ch, miss 1 st; rep from * to end, sl st into first tr.

17th round: Sl st into next tr, *22tr, 2tr into next st, 2tr into sp, 1ch, 1tr, 5ch, miss 1 st; rep from * to end, sl st into first tr.

18th round: Sl st into next tr, *24tr, 4ch, 1dc into 4ch sp, 4ch, miss 1 st; rep from * to end, sl st into first tr.

19th round: Sl st into next tr, *21tr, 5ch, 2tr in next sp, 1tr into next dc, 2tr in next sp, 5ch, miss 1 st; rep from * to end, sl st into first tr.

20th round: Sl st into next tr, *18tr, 5ch, 3tr into next sp, 2tr into next tr, 8ch, miss 3tr, 2tr into next st, 3tr into next sp, 5ch, miss tr; rep from * to end, sl st into first tr.

21st round: Sl st into next tr, *15tr, 5ch, 3tr into next sp, 2tr into next tr, 5ch, 1dc into next sp, 5ch, miss 4tr, 2tr in next tr, 3tr into next sp, 5ch, miss 1tr; rep from * to end, sl st into first tr.

22nd round: Sl st into next tr, *12tr, 5ch, 3tr into next sp, 2tr into next tr, 5ch, 1dc into next sp, 1dc into next dc, 1dc into next sp, 5ch, miss 4tr, 2tr into next tr, 3tr into next sp, 5ch, miss 1tr; rep from * to end, sl st into first tr.

23rd round: Sl st into next tr, *9tr, 5ch, 3tr into next sp, 2tr into next tr, 6ch, 1dc into next sp, 1dc into each of next 3dc, 1dc into next sp, 6ch, miss 4tr, 2tr into next tr, 3tr into next sp, 5ch, miss 1tr; rep from * to end, sl st into first tr.

24th round: Sl st into next tr, *6tr, 5ch,

3tr into next sp, 2tr in next tr, 8ch, miss 3tr, 2tr in next st, 3tr into sp, 7ch, miss 1dc, 1dc into each of next 3dc, 7ch, rep from ** to ** once more, 5ch, miss 1tr; rep from * to end, sl st into first tr.

25th round: Sl st into next tr, *3tr, 5ch, **3tr into next sp, 2tr into next st, 5ch, 1dc into next sp, 5ch, miss 4tr, 2tr in next tr, 3tr in sp**, 7ch, miss 1dc, 1dc into next dc, 7ch; rep from ** to ** once, 5ch, miss 1tr; rep from * to end, sl st into first tr.

26th round: Sl st into next tr, *1ttr into next tr, 1ch, **3tr in next sp, 2tr in next tr, 5ch, 1dc in arch, 1dc into next dc, 1dc in arch, 5ch, miss 4tr, 2tr in next tr, 3tr in arch**, 2ch; rep from ** to ** once, 1ch, miss 1tr; rep from * to end, sl st into first tr.

27th round: *1tr, 1tr in next sp, **1tr, 6ch, 1dc into arch, 1 dc into each of next 3dc, 1dc into arch, 6ch, miss 4tr, 1tr, ** 3tr into next arch; rep from ** to ** once, 1tr into next sp; rep from * to end, sl st into first tr.

28th round: Sl st into each of next 2tr, *[2tr in next tr, 3tr into next arch, 7ch, miss 1dc, 1dc into each of next 3dc, 7ch, 3tr into next arch, 2tr into next tr**, 6ch, miss 3tr; rep from * to ** once, 9ch, miss 3tr; rep from * to end, sl st into first tr.

29th round: Sl st into each of next 4tr, *2tr into next tr, 3tr into next arch, 7ch, miss 1dc, 1dc into next dc, 7ch, 3tr into next arch, 2tr into next tr**, 6ch, 1dc into next arch, 6ch; rep from * to ** once, 5ch, 1dc into next arch, 5ch, miss 4tr; rep from * to end, sl st into first tr.

30th round: Sl st into each of next 4tr, *2tr into next tr, 3tr into next arch, 2ch, 3tr into next arch, 2tr into next tr**, [7ch, 1dc into next arch] twice, 7ch, miss 4tr; rep from * to ** once, 5ch, 1dc into next arch, 1dc into next dc, 1dc in next arch, 5ch, miss 4tr; rep from * to end, sl st into first tr.

31st round: Sl st into each of next 4tr, *1tr, 3tr into next arch, 1tr, [7ch, 1dc into next arch] 3 times, 7ch, miss 4tr, 1tr, 3tr into next arch, 1tr, 6ch, 1dc into next arch, 1dc into each of next 3dc, 1dc into next arch, 6ch, miss 4tr; rep from * to end, sl st into first tr.

32nd round: *2tr into same st as sl st of previous row [8ch, 1dc into next arch] 4 times, 8ch, miss 4tr, 2tr into next tr, 3tr into next sp, 7ch, miss 1dc, 1dc into each of next 3dc, 7ch, 3tr into next sp; rep from * to end, sl st into first tr.

33rd round: Sl st to centre of first arch, *[1dc into arch, 8ch] 5 times, miss 4tr, 2tr into next tr, 3tr into next arch, 7ch, miss 1dc, 1dc into next dc, 7ch, 3tr into next arch, 2tr into next tr, 8ch; rep from * to end, sl st into first dc.

34th round: Sl st to centre of first arch, *[1dc into arch, 9ch] 5 times, miss 4tr, 2tr into next tr, 3tr into next arch, 2ch, 3tr into next arch, 2tr into next tr, 9ch, 1dc into next arch, 9ch; rep from * to end, sl st into first tr.

35th round: Sl st to centre of first arch, *[1dc into arch, 9ch] 5 times, miss 4tr, 1tr, [9ch, 1dc into next arch] twice, 9ch; rep from * to end, sl st into first dc.

36th round: Sl st to centre of first arch, *1dc into arch, 10ch; rep from * to end, sl st into first dc.

37th round: 14dc into each arch to end, sl st into first dc.

Fasten off.

— ◆ —

17

Place Mat with Hearts

✪✪✪

Materials

Coats Patons Opera No. 20 Crochet Cotton Shade 500 - 150 grams

1.00mm Milward Steel Crochet Hook

1 reel Sylko Sewing Thread

1 sewing needle

26 cm x 60 cm piece of white linen

Note

On each side of the Place Mat, the edging is made up of 8 hearts worked separately and then sewn together at the sides using small stitches. Eight stems and two spikes are made separately and finally sewn on the crochet net.

Hearts

Make 5ch, into 5th ch from hook work [2tr, 1ch] twice, 1tr, turn. (1tr, 1ch) at beg of row.

1st row: 4ch (count as 1tr, 1ch), *2tr into next sp, 1ch; rep from * twice more, 1tr into 3rd of 4ch.

2nd row: 4ch (count as 1tr, 1ch), [1tr 1ch, 2tr] into first sp, *1ch, 2tr into next sp; rep from * to end, 1ch, 1tr into 3rd of 4ch, turn.

3rd row: as 2nd row.

4th row: 4ch, 2tr into first sp, 1ch, *2tr into next sp, 1ch; rep from * to end, 1tr into 3rd of 4ch, turn.

5th, 6th and 7th rows: As 4th row.

8th row: 3ch, 1tr into first ch, 1ch, *2tr into next sp, 1ch; rep from * to last sp, 1tr into last sp, 1tr into 3rd of 4ch, turn.

9th row: 4ch, *2tr into next sp, 1ch; rep from * to end, 1tr into 3rd of 3ch, turn.

10th, 11th, 12th and 13th rows: Rep the last 2 rows twice more.

14th row: 3ch, miss 1sp, [2tr, 1ch into next 1chsp] 5 times, 3ch, 1dc between next 2tr, 3ch, [2tr, 1ch into next 1chsp] 4 times, 2tr into next sp, 1tr into 3rd of 4ch, turn.

15th row: 3ch, *2tr into next 1chsp, 1ch rep from * twice, 2tr into next 1chsp, 1tr into 3rd of 3ch, turn.

16th row: 3ch, [2tr, 1ch into next 1chsp] twice, 2tr into next 1chsp, 1tr into 3rd of 3ch. Fasten off.

Rejoin yarn to free chsp and complete other side of top of heart to match first side, then continue in dc around heart as follows:

1st round (right side): 3dc into each sp and each row round edge of heart working 3dc at lower point, sl st into first dc.

2nd round: Work 1dc into each dc and 3dc into centre dc at point, sl st into first dc.

Fasten off.

Make 7 more hearts in the same way, then join them in a row by sewing together 8dc level with 10th, 11th and 12th rows at the side of one heart to the corresponding 8dc on the adjoining heart.

Upper Arches

Fill in spaces between each heart as follows:

1st row: Rejoin yarn with a sl st into 2nd free dc of one left side of heart, 5ch, 1dc into 2nd free dc of side of adjacent heart, sl st into each of next 3dc, turn.

2nd row: 5ch, 1dc into first arch, 5ch, miss 1dc on side of first heart, sl st into each of next 3dc, turn.

3rd row: [5ch, 1dc into next arch] twice, 5ch, miss 1dc on 2nd heart, sl st into next dc.

Fasten off.

Work these three rows between remaining hearts.

Straighten outside edges as folows:

Rejoin yarn with a sl st into dc level with the 12th row of first heart, 8ch, miss next 3dc on heart, sl st into each of next 3dc, turn, 5ch, 1dc into 8ch arch, 2ch, 1htr into 3rd of 8ch.

Fasten off.

Work on outside edge of last heart in the same way, turn but do not fasten off at end.

Continuing along top of hearts and arches, work as follows:

1st row: 1ch, 1dc into htr, 5ch, 1dc into next arch, *5ch, miss 2dc on heart, [1dc into next dc, 5ch, miss 3dc] 3 times, tr2tog (working first st into next dc missing 10dc and 2nd st into next dc), 5ch, miss 2dc, [1dc into next dc, 5ch, miss 3dc] twice, 1dc into next dc, [5ch, 1dc into next arch] 3 times; rep from * to end, turn.

This versatile cloth could be used as a placemat or napkin, and is robust enough to take on an al fresco picnic.

2nd row: 7ch (count as 1htr, 5ch), miss first arch, *1dc into next arch, 5ch; rep from * to end, 1dc into last arch, turn.

Rep 2nd row 10 times more.

Fasten off.

Lower Arches

Fill in spaces between each heart as follows:

1st row: Rejoin yarn with a sl st into 4th free dc on left side of first heart, 5ch, miss 3dc on side of adjacent heart, sl st into each of next 3dc, turn.

2nd row: 5ch, 1dc into arch, 5ch, miss 2dc on first heart, sl st into each of next 3dc, turn.

3rd row: [5ch, 1dc into next arch] twice, 5ch, miss 2dc, on 2nd heart, sl st into each of next 3dc, turn.

4th row: [5ch, 1dc into next arch] 3 times, 5ch, miss 2dc, sl st into each of next 3dc, turn.

5th row: [5ch, 1dc into next arch] 4 times, 5ch, miss 2dc, sl st into each of next 3dc, turn.

6th row: [5ch, 1dc into next arch] 5 times, 5ch, miss 2dc, sl st into each of next 3dc, turn.

7th row: [5ch, 1dc into next arch] 6 times, 5ch, miss 2dc, sl st into each of next 3dc, turn.

8th row: [5ch, 1dc into next arch] 7 times, 5ch, miss 2dc, sl st into each of next 3dc, turn.

9th row: [5ch, 1dc into next arch] 8 times, 5ch, miss 2dc, sl st into each of next 3dc, turn.

10th row: [5ch, 1dc into next arch] 9 times, 5ch, sl st into point of adjacent heart.

Fasten off.

Work these 10 rows between remaining hearts, then work on outside edges as follows:

Work as for upper outside edge, then continue working 1 more arch on every row until 10 rows have been completed.

Fasten off.

Now work each scallop separately.

1st row: Rejoin yarn with a dc into 10th arch from side edge [5ch, 1dc into next arch] 8 times, 2ch, 1tr into next arch, turn.

2nd row: 7ch, [1dc into next arch, 5ch] 6 times, 1dc into next arch, 2ch, 1tr into next arch, turn.

3rd row: 7ch, [1dc into next arch, 5ch] 5 times, 1dc into next arch, 2ch, 1tr into next arch, turn.

4th row: [5ch, 1dc into next arch] 5 times, 1ch, 1tr into next arch, turn.

5th row: [2ch, 1dc into next arch] 5 times.

Fasten off.

Work these 5 rows for the remaining 7 scallops.

Outer Edging

With right side facing rejoin yarn with a sl st into top right hand corner and work as follows:

1st round: 1dc into corner arch, *2ch, 1dc into next arch; rep from * along top edge, work 4dc into each row of arches and 1dc into each dc down left side edge, 4dc into each arch on scalloped edge, then 4dc into each row of arches and 1dc into each dc up right front edge, sl st into first dc.

Working 3dc into each sp at top edge and 1dc into each dc on remaining 3 sides, continue as follows

2nd round: *3dc, 1 picot (see Special Abbreviations on page 5); rep from * to end, sl st into first dc.

Fasten off.

Stem (Make 4)

Make 85ch and work 1dc into 2nd ch from hook, 1dc into each ch to end.

Fasten off.

Bar

Make 361ch, 1dc into 2nd ch from hook, 1dc into each ch to end.

Fasten off.

Sew the stem joining the hearts in pairs as shown in the photograph. Sew the scalloped bar passing through the loops made by the stems as illustrated.

Make another piece exactly the same for other side of Mat

For remainng 2 sides of mat work 2 lengths of edging as follows:

Make 131ch, 1dc into 2nd ch from hook, 1dc into each of next 2ch, 1 picot, *1dc into each of next 3ch, 1 picot; rep from * to last ch, 3dc into last ch, do not turn but continue along other side of foundation ch in the same way, sl st into first dc.

Fasten off.

Making Up

Make a zig-zag all round the fabric. Leaving the picots free sew the two edgings to the long sides of the fabric. Sew the two narrow edgings to the short sides of the fabric.

18
Diamond Filet Curtain

✪✪✪

Materials

Coats Patons Musica No. 5 Crochet Cotton Shade 500 - 100 grams
1.75mm Milward Steel Crochet Hook

Note:

This attractive Diamond Filet Curtain pattern could be added to the edge of a tablecloth or to a pair of curtains as a border.

To Make

Make 135ch.

1st row: 1tr into 4th ch from hook, 1tr into each of next 3ch (1blk worked at beg of row), [2ch, miss 2ch, 1tr into next tr] 3 times (3sps), 5ch, miss 5ch, 1tr into next ch, 1tr into each of next 4tr (2sp-bar and 1 blk), 5ch, miss 5ch, 1tr into next tr (2sp-bar), [2ch, miss 2ch, 1tr into next ch] 3 times (3sps), 1tr into each of next 3tr, [2ch, miss 2ch, 1tr into next tr] 8 times, (8sps), *1tr into each of next 3tr, 2ch, miss 2ch, 1tr into each of next 4ch, 8ch, miss 8ch (1blk, 1sp, 1blk and a sp-bar); rep from * once more, 1ch into each of next 16tr (5 blks), 8ch, miss 8ch, 1tr into each of next 4ch, 2ch, miss 2ch, 1tr into each of last 4ch (3sp-bar, 1 blk, 1sp, 1blk), turn. 44 squares.

TIP

In crochet when decreasing stitches on the sides, miss the second and the penultimate stitch instead of the first and the last one so that it will show less.

18

Keep your privacy and enhance the look of your kitchen with this pretty
curtain. Don't worry - you won't lose any light as the filet can't
stop the sun from pouring in!

2nd row: Sl st across first 4tr (1 blk decreased), 3ch (count as 1tr), 2tr into sp (1blk over 1sp), 2ch, miss 2tr, 1tr into next tr (1sp over 1 blk), 2tr into 3sp-bar, 5ch, 1tr into each of next 16tr (1 blk and a sp bar over a 3sp bar and 5 blks over 5 blks), 2sp-bar and 1 blk over 3sp-bar, 1sp, 1 blk, 2sp-bar, 1 blk, 2sp-bar, 1 blk, 1sp, 1 blk, 7sps, 1 blk, 4sps, 3sp-bar, 4sps, 1 blk placing last tr into 3rd of 3ch, turn.

Continue in this way following chart to end.

Rep these 60 rows 5 times more (or for the required length), then rep first 35 rows again.

Fasten off.

Edging

Rejoin yarn to top corner of last row. Working along side edge and replacing every 2tr by a picot (see Special Abbreviations on page 5), work 1tr into each tr and 2tr into each sp to next corner. Continue along shaped edge working 2tr into first row, *1tr into each of next 3 sts, 1 picot, 2tr into next row; rep from * to starting ch, then work along other side edge as for first.

Fasten off.

Key |■| = Block |‾| = Space |___| = 2 Space Bar |___| = 3 Space Bar |◡| = Lacet

WOODLAND HUES

19

The doilies featured here and on page 49 are useful for protecting your delicate wooden surfaces and would work well as a base for all the paraphenalia of the dressing table.

19

Star and Flower Doily

✪

Materials

Coats Patons Opera No. 20 Crochet Cotton Shade 500 - 50 grams

1.00mm Milward Steel Crochet Hook

To Make

Make 6ch, join into a ring with a sl st.

1st round: Work 16dc into ring, sl st into first dc.

2nd round: 6ch (count as 1tr, 3ch), miss first 2dc, *1tr, 3ch, miss 1dc; rep from * to end, sl st into 3rd of 6ch.

3rd round: Sl st into chsp, 6ch (count as 1 quadtr), quad4trtog, 8ch, *quad5trtog into chsp, 8ch; rep from * to end, sl st into 6th of 6ch.

4th round: Sl st into next sp, 12dc into each 8chsp to end, sl st into first dc.

5th round: 1dc into **back loop only** of each st to end, sl st into first dc.

6th, 7th and 8th rounds: As 5th round.

9th round: 1dc into first dc, 5ch, miss 2 sts, *1dc into next dc, 5ch, miss 2 sts; rep from * to end, sl st into first dc.

10th round: Sl st to centre of 5chsp, 1dc into same sp, 5ch, *1dc into next 5chsp, 5ch; rep from * to end, sl st into first dc.

11th round: As 10th round.

12th round: Sl st to centre of 5chsp, 1dc into same sp, 6ch, *1dc into next 5chsp, 6ch; rep from * to end, sl st into first dc.

13th round: Sl st into centre of 6chsp, *3dc into sp, 5ch, *[1dc into next chsp, 7ch] twice, 1dc into next chsp, 5ch; rep from * to end, sl st into first dc.

14th round: 1dc into each of first 3dc, *2dc into next sp, [7ch, 1dc into next sp] twice, 7ch, 2dc into next sp, 1dc into each of next 3dc; rep from * 7 times, omitting 3dc at end of last rep, sl st into first dc.

15th round: 1dc into each of first 5dc, *3dc into next sp, 7ch, 1dc into next sp, 7ch, 3dc into next sp, 1dc into each of next 7dc; rep from * 6 times, 3dc into next sp, 7ch, 1dc into next sp, 7ch, 3dc into next sp, 1dc into each of last 2dc, sl st into first dc.

Working 1dc into each dc unless otherwise indicated, continue as follows:

16th round: 8dc, *3dc into next sp, 7ch, 3dc into next space, 13dc; rep from * 6 times, 3dc into next sp, 7ch, 3dc into next space, 5dc, sl st into first dc.

17th round: 11dc, *[2dc, 3ch, 2dc] into next sp, 19dc; rep from * 6 times, [2dc, 3ch, 3dc] into next sp, 8dc, sl st into first dc.

18th round: 13dc, 5dc into 3chsp, *23dc, 5dc into next 3chsp; rep from * 6 times, 10dc, sl st into first dc.

19th round: 1dc into each dc to end, sl st into first dc.

20th round: Sl st into each of first 3dc, 6ch (count as 1tr, 3ch), 1tr into next st, **(centre of curve)** *11ch, miss 9sts, 1dc, 7ch, miss 3 sts; [1tr, 3ch, 1tr] into next st **(point)**, 7ch, miss 3 sts, 1dc, 11ch, miss 9 sts, [1tr, 3ch, 1tr] in next st; rep from * 7 times omitting [1tr, 3ch, 1tr] at end of last rep, sl st into 3rd of 3ch.

21st round: Sl st into sp, 6ch (count as 1tr, 3ch), 1tr into next st, *12ch, 1dc into dc, 7ch, 1tr into tr, [1tr, 1 picot (see Special Abbreviations on page 5) 1tr] into sp, 1tr into tr, 7ch, 1dc into dc, 12ch, [1tr, 3ch, 1tr] into sp; rep from * 7 times omitting [1tr, 3ch, 1tr] at end of last rep, sl st into 3rd of 6ch.

Fasten off.

TIP

To fasten off, cut the working thread to approximately 10cm (4in), pass it through the last crochet stitch and pull firmly.

20

Floral Doily

✿✿

Materials

Coats Patons Opera No. 20 Crochet Cotton Shade 500 - 50 grams

1.00mm Milward Steel Crochet Hook

To Make

Make 10ch, join into a ring with a sl st.

1st round: 3ch (count as 1tr), work 23tr into ring, sl st into 3rd of 3ch.

2nd round: 1dc into same st as last sl st, 4ch, miss 1tr, *1dc into next tr, 4ch, miss 1 st; rep from * to end, sl st into first dc.

3rd round: Sl st to centre of 4ch arch, 1dc into same arch as last sl st, 5ch, *1dc in next arch, 5ch; rep from * to end, sl st into first dc.

4th round: Sl st into first arch, 3ch (count as 1tr), [3tr, 1ch, 1tr, 1ch, 4tr] into same arch as last sl st, 3ch *miss 1 arch, [4tr, 1ch, 1tr, 1ch, 4tr] into next arch, 3ch; rep from * to end, sl st into 3rd of 3ch.

5th round: 3ch, tr3tog over next 3 sts, 3ch, 4tr into next tr, 3ch, tr4tog over next 4 sts, 4ch, miss 1 arch, *tr4tog over next 4 sts, 3ch, 4tr into next tr, 3ch, tr4tog over next 4 sts, 4ch, miss 1 arch; rep from * to end, sl st into top of tr3tog.

6th round: Sl st into first arch, 1dc into same arch as sl st, 5ch, tr4tog over next 4tr, [5ch, 1dc into next arch] twice, 5ch, *1dc into next arch, 5ch, tr4tog over next 4tr, [5ch, 1dc into next arch] twice, 5ch; rep from * to end, sl st into first dc.

7th round: Sl st to centre of first arch, 1dc into same arch as sl st, 6ch, *1dc into next arch, 6ch; rep from * to end, sl st into first dc.

8th round: As 7th round.

9th round: Sl st to centre of first arch, 1dc into same arch as sl st, 7ch, *1dc into next arch, 7ch; rep from * to end, sl st into first dc.

10th round: Sl st into first arch, 3ch (count as 1tr), 3tr into same arch as sl st, 5ch, 1dc into next arch, 5ch, *4tr into next arch, 5ch, 1dc into next arch, 5ch; rep from * to end, sl st into 3rd of 3ch.

11th round: Sl st to first arch, 3ch, 3tr into same arch as sl st, 5ch, *4tr into next arch, 5ch; rep from * to end, sl st into 3rd of 3ch.

12th round: Sl st into next 3tr, 3ch, *[3tr, 1ch, 3tr] into next arch, 1tr into

48

next tr, 4ch, 3dc into next arch, 4ch, miss 3tr, 1tr into next tr; rep from * to end omitting 1tr at end of last rep, sl st into 3rd of 3ch.

13th round: Sl st into next tr, 3ch, 1tr into next tr, *2tr into next 1chsp, 1tr into each of next 2tr, 4ch, 1dc into next arch, 1dc into each of next 3dc, 1dc into next arch, 4ch, miss 2tr, 1tr into each of next 2tr; rep from * to end omitting 2tr at end of last rep, sl st into 3rd of 3ch.

Working 1tr into each tr unless otherwise indicated, continue as follows:
14th round: Sl st into next tr, 3ch, 3tr, *4ch, 1dc into next arch, 5dc, 1dc into next arch, 4ch, miss 1tr, 4tr; rep from * to end omitting 4tr at end of last rep, sl st into 3rd of 3ch.

15th round: Sl st into next 3tr, 3ch, *3tr into next arch, 4ch, miss 1dc, 1dc into each of next 5dc, 4ch, 3tr into next arch, 1tr into next tr, 5ch, miss 2tr, 1tr; rep from * to end omitting 1tr at end of last rep, sl st into 3rd of 3ch.

16th round: Sl st into each of next 3tr, 3ch, *3tr into next arch, 5ch, miss 1dc, 3dc, 5ch, 3tr into next arch, 1tr into next tr, 4ch, 3dc into next arch, 4ch, miss 3tr, 1tr; rep from * to end omitting 1tr at end of last rep, sl st into 3rd of 3ch.

17th round: Sl st into each of next 3tr, 3ch, *3tr into next arch, 2ch, 3tr into next arch, 1tr into next tr, 5ch, 1dc into next arch, 3dc, 1dc into next arch, 5ch, miss 3tr, 1tr; rep from * to end omitting 1tr at end of last rep, sl st into 3rd of 3ch.

18th round: Sl st into each of next 2tr, 3ch, 1tr, *2tr into next arch, 2tr, 5ch, 1dc into next arch, 5dc, 1dc into next arch, 5ch, miss 2tr, 2tr; rep from * to end omitting 2tr at end of last rep, sl st into 3rd of 3ch.

19th round: Sl st into next 5tr, 3ch, *3tr into next arch, 4ch, miss 1dc, 5dc, 4ch, 3tr into next arch, 2ch, miss 4tr, 1tr; rep from * to end omitting 1tr at end of last rep, sl st into 3rd of 3ch.

20th round: Sl st into each of next 3tr, 3ch, *3tr into next arch, 4ch, miss 1dc, 3dc, 4ch, 3tr into next arch, 1tr, 5ch, 2tr into next arch, 5ch, miss 3tr, 1tr; rep from * to end omitting 1tr at end of last rep, sl st into 3rd of 3ch.

21st round: Sl st into each of next 3tr, 3ch, *3tr into next arch, 2ch, 3tr into next arch, 1tr into next tr, 6ch, 2tr, 6ch, miss 3tr, 1tr; rep from * to end omitting 1tr at end of last rep, sl st into 3rd of 3ch.

22nd round: Sl st into each of next 2tr, 3ch, 1tr, *2tr in next arch, 2tr, 8ch, miss 2tr, 2tr into next tr, 2ch, 2tr into next tr, 8ch, miss 2tr, 2tr; rep from * to end omitting 2tr at end of last rep, sl st into 3rd of 3ch.

23rd round: Sl st into next tr, 3ch, 3tr, *9ch, miss 1tr, 2tr into next tr, 1tr, 2ch, 1tr into next arch, 2ch, 1tr, 2tr into next

tr, 9ch, miss 1tr, 4tr; rep from * to end omitting 4tr at end of last rep, sl st into 3rd of 3ch.

24th round: Sl st into next tr, 3ch, 1tr, *9ch, miss 1tr, 2tr into next tr, 2tr, 2ch, [1tr, 2ch, 1tr] into next tr, 2ch, 2tr, 2tr into next tr, 9ch, miss 1tr, 2tr; rep from * to end omitting 2tr at end of last rep, sl st into 3rd of 3ch.

25th round: 3ch, 1tr, *9ch, 4tr, [2ch, 1tr into next tr] twice, 2ch, 4tr, 9ch, 2tr; rep from * to end omitting 2tr at end of last rep, sl st into 3rd of 3ch.

26th round: 3ch, 1tr, *9ch, tr4tog over next 4tr, 2ch, 2tr into sp, 1tr, 2ch, 1tr into next sp, 2ch, 1tr, 2tr into next sp, 2ch, tr4tog over next 4tr, 9ch, 2tr; rep from * to end omitting 2tr at end of last rep, sl st into 3rd of 3ch.

27th round: 3ch, 1tr, *9ch, miss next st, 2tr into next tr, 2tr, 2ch, [1tr, 2ch, 1tr] into next tr, 2ch, 2tr, 2tr into next tr, 9ch, 2tr; rep from * to end omitting 2tr at end of last rep, sl st into 3rd of 3ch.

28th round: 3ch, 1tr into same st as last sl st, *2ch, 2tr into next tr, 9ch, 4tr, [2ch, 1tr into next tr] twice, 2ch, 4tr, 9ch, 2tr into next tr; rep from * to end omitting 2tr at end of last rep, sl st into 3rd of 3ch.

29th round: 3ch, 1tr into same st as last sl st, *1tr, 2ch, 1tr into next sp, 2ch, 1tr, 2tr into next tr, 9ch, tr4tog over next 4tr, 2ch, 2tr into next sp, 1tr, 2ch, 1tr into next sp, 2ch, 1tr into next tr, 2tr into next sp, 2ch, tr4tog over 4tr, 9ch, 2tr into next st; rep from * to end omitting 2tr at end of last rep, sl st into 3rd of 3ch.

Working first tr as 3ch, continue as follows:
30th round: *2tr into next tr, 2tr, 2ch, [1tr, 2ch, 1tr] into next tr, 2ch, 2tr, 2tr into next tr, 9ch; rep from * to end, sl st into first tr.

31st round: *4tr, [2ch, 1tr] twice, 2ch, 4tr, 7ch; rep from * to end, sl st into first tr.

32nd round: 1tr, tr3tog over next 3tr, *4ch, miss next sp, 2tr into next sp, 4ch, tr4tog over next 4tr, 9ch, tr4tog over next 4tr; rep from * to end omitting tr4tog at end of last rep, sl st into top of tr3tog.

33rd round: 2tr into same st as last sl st, *4ch, 1tr into next arch, 2tr, 1tr into next arch, 4ch, 2tr into next st, 9tr into next arch, 2tr into next st; rep from * to end omitting 2tr at end of last rep, sl st into first tr.

34th round: *1tr, 2tr into next tr, 2ch, 4tr, 2ch, 2tr into next tr, 10tr; rep from * to end, sl st into first tr.

35th round: *2tr, 2tr into next tr, 2ch, tr4tog over next 4tr, 2ch, 2tr into next tr, 11tr; rep from * to end, sl st into first tr.

36th round: *3tr, 2tr into next tr, 2ch, 1tr into next st, 2ch, 2tr into next tr, 12tr; rep from * to end, sl st into first tr.

37th round: *4tr, 2tr into next tr, 2ch, miss 1tr, 2tr into next tr, 13tr; rep from * to end, sl st into first tr.

38th round: *6tr, 2tr into next sp, 15tr; rep from * to end, sl st into first tr.

39th round: 1dc into same st as last sl st, 7ch, miss 4tr, *1dc into next tr, 7ch, miss 4tr; rep from * to end, sl st into first dc.

40th round: Sl st to centre of first arch, *1dc into arch, 7ch; rep from * to end, sl st into first dc.

41st round: Sl st into first arch, [4tr, 2ch, 1tr, 2ch, 4tr] into same arch, 1dc into next arch, *[4tr, 2ch, 1tr, 2ch, 4tr] into next arch, 1dc into next arch; rep from * to end, sl st into first tr.

42nd round: *tr4tog over 4tr, 3ch, 4tr into next tr, 3ch, tr4tog over 4tr; rep from * to end, sl st into first st.

43rd round: 1dc into same st as last sl st, 6ch, tr4tog over next 4tr, 6ch, miss next st, 1dc into next st; rep from * to end omitting 1dc at end of last rep, sl st into first dc.

44th round: Sl st into first arch, 7dc into same arch, *[1dc, 1 picot (see Special Abbreviation on page 5), 1dc] in next st, 7dc into each of next 2 arches; rep from * to end omitting 7dc, at end of last rep, sl st into first dc.

Fasten off.

—— ◆ ——

21
Ornate Curtain
✪✪✪

Materials
Coats Patons Musica No. 5 Crochet Cotton Shade 503 - 200 grams
1.75mm Milward Steel Crochet Hook

First Large Motif
Make 14ch, join into a ring with a sl st.

1st round: Work 24dc into ring, sl st into first dc.

2nd round: 7ch (count as 1dtr, 3ch), miss first 2dc, *1dtr into next dc, 3ch, miss 1dc; rep from * to end, sl st into 4th of 7ch.

3rd round: Sl st into first sp, [2dc,

1 picot (see Special Abbreviations on page 5), 2dc] into same sp as last sl st, *[2dc, 1 picot, 2dc] into next sp; rep from * to end, sl st into first dc.

4th round: *18ch (count as 1dtr, 14ch), miss first 8dc, *1dtr into next dc, 14ch, miss 7dc; rep from * to end, sl st into 4th of 18ch.

5th round: Sl st into first sp, 17dc into same sp as last sl st, *17dc into next sp; rep from * to end, sl st into first dc.

Working first dc of each round in same st as previous sl st and 1dc into each dc unless otherwise indicated, continue as follows:

6th round: Sl st into next dc, *15dc, 3ch, miss 2dc; rep from * to end, sl st into first dc.

7th round: Sl st into next dc, *13dc, 3ch, 1dc into next sp, 3ch, miss 1dc; rep from * to end, sl st into first dc.

8th round: Sl st into next dc, *11dc, [3ch, 1dc into next arch] twice, 3ch, miss 1dc; rep from * to end, sl st into first dc.

9th round: Sl st into next dc, 1dc into same st as last sl st, *9dc, 3ch, 1dc into next arch, 8ch, miss 1 arch, 1dc into next arch, 3ch, miss 1dc; rep from * to end, sl st into first dc.

10th round: Sl st into next dc, 1dc, *7dc, 3ch, 1dc into next arch, [2dc, 1 picot] 4 times and 2dc into 8ch arch, 1dc into next arch, 3ch, miss 1dc; rep from * to end, sl st into first dc.

11th round: Sl st into next dc, 1dc, *5dc, 3ch, 1dc into next arch, 8ch, 1dc into 2nd picot, 2ch, 1dc into next picot, 8ch, 1dc into next arch, 3ch, miss 1dc; rep from * to end, sl st into first dc.

12th round: Sl st into next dc, 1dc, *3dc, 3ch, 1dc into next arch, **[2dc, 1 picot] 4 times and 2dc into 8ch arch**, 2dc into 2chsp; rep from ** to ** once, 1dc into next arch, 3ch, miss 1dc; rep from * to end, sl st into first dc.

13th round: Sl st into next dc, 1dc, *3ch, 1dc into next arch, 8ch, 1dc into 2nd picot, 2ch, 1dc into next picot, 10ch, 1dc into 2nd picot, 2ch, 1dc into next picot, 8ch, 1dc into next arch, 3ch, miss 1dc, 1dc into next dc; rep from * to end omitting 1dc at end of last rep, sl st into first dc.

14th round: Sl st into centre of first arch, 1dc into same arch, *[2dc, 1 picot] 4 times and 2dc into 8ch arch, 2dc into 2chsp, [2dc, 1 picot] 5 times and 2dc into 10ch arch, 2dc into 2chsp, [2dc, 1 picot] 4 times and 2dc into next 8ch arch, 1dc into next arch, 3ch, 1dc into next arch; rep from * to end omitting 1dc at end of last rep, sl st into first dc. Fasten off.

2nd Large Motif

Work first 13 rounds as given for First Motif, then join as follows:

14th round: Sl st to centre of first arch, 1dc into same arch, [2dc, 1 picot] 4 times and 2dc into first 8ch arch, 2dc into next sp, into next 10ch arch work [2dc, 1 picot, 2dc, 1 picot, 2dc, 1 joining picot into 3rd picot of a 10ch arch on first motif, 2dc, *1 joining picot into next picot on first motif, 2dc, rep from * once more], 2dc into next sp, into next 8ch arch work [2dc *1 joining picot into next picot on first motif, 2dc, rep from * twice more, 1 picot, 2dc], 1dc into next arch, 3ch, 1dc into next arch, into next 8ch arch work [2dc, 1 picot, 2dc, miss next picot on first motif, 1 joining picot into next picot, 2dc, *1 joining picot into next picot on first motif, 2dc, rep from * once more], 2dc into next sp, into next 10ch arch work [2dc, *1 joining picot into next picot on first motif, 2dc, rep from * twice more, 1 picot, 2dc, 1 picot, 2dc], 2dc into next sp, then complete round as for first motif.

Work 4 more motifs in this way, joining them in a row as for 2nd motif.

Work another row of 6 motifs as before but joining them to the corresponding motif of first row by joining the last 5 picots of 14th round to 5 picots of first row motif (see photograph).

Small Filling Motifs

Make 14ch, join into a ring with a sl st.

1st round: Work 24dc into ring, sl st into first dc.

2nd round: 6ch (count as 1tr, 3ch), miss first 2dc, *1tr into next dc, 3ch, miss 1dc; rep from * to end, sl st into 3rd of 6ch.

3rd round: Sl st into first sp [2dc, 1 picot, 2dc] into same sp as last sl st, *[2dc, 1 picot, 2dc] into next sp; rep from * to end, sl st into first dc.

4th round: 1dc into same st as last sl st, 8ch, miss 6dc, *1dc into next dc, 8ch, miss 6dc, 1dc into next dc; rep from * to end, sl st into first dc.

5th round: Sl st into first arch, into same arch work [2dc, 1 picot, 2dc, 1 joining picot into the free picot of 2nd Large Motif immediately before the 3 joining picots of 2 motifs, 2dc, 1 joining picot into first free picot after the 3 joining picots, 2dc, 1 picot, 2dc], into each of next 2 arches work [2dc, 1 picot] 4 times and 2dc, turn, [8ch, miss 1 picot on next arch, 1dc into next picot, 2ch, 1dc into next picot, 8ch, miss 3dc, 1dc into each of next 2dc] twice, turn, sl st into last 8ch arch formed, into same arch work *[2dc, 1 picot, 2dc, 1 joining picot into 2nd picot of next arch of first motif, 2dc, 1 joining picot into next picot, 2dc, 1 picot, 2dc]*, rep from * to * into next 8ch arch working the joining picots into 2nd and 3rd picots on next arch of first motif, then rep from * to * twice more into next 2 8ch arches working joining picots into 2nd and 3rd picots of each of the 2 free arches on next motif above first, then complete other

half of small filling motif to match first half.

Work remaining 4 inner filling motifs in the same way.

Work 5 more upper filling motifs as the inner filling motifs but working into 2 arches only on large motifs (see photograph).

Joining Side Arches

With wrong side facing rejoin yarn with a dc into first dc before the 5 joining picots at one side edge, 7ch, 1dc into the first dc after the 5 joining picots, turn [2dc, 1 picot] 3 times and 2dc into 7chsp. Fasten off.

With wrong side facing rejoin yarn with a dc into 2nd picot of first arch of next 3 arch free scallop of large motif, 4ch, miss 2 picot, 1dc into next picot, 8ch, 1dc into centre picot of previous side 7ch arch, 8ch, miss 3 picots, 1dc into next picot, 4ch, miss 2 picots, 1dc into next picot, turn, 4dc into next 4ch arch, into each of next 2 8ch arches, work [2dc, 1 picot] 4 times and 2dc, 4dc into next 4ch arch, sl st to next picot, turn 1dc into same picots as last sl st, *8ch, miss 1 picot, 1dc into next picot*, 8ch, miss 4 picot, 1dc into next picot; rep from * to * turn, into each of the 3 8ch arches work [2dc, 1 picot] 4 times and 2dc. Fasten off.

Work filling arches in the same way on the other side edge.

Corner Filling Arches

With wrong side facing rejoin yarn with a dc into last joining picot between large and small motifs, 8ch, miss 1 picot [1dc into next picot, 1ch] 4 times, 1dc into next picot, 8ch, miss 1 picot, 1dc into next picot, 1ch, 1dc into next picot, turn, 1dc into chsp, [2dc, 1 picot] 4 times and 2dc into next arch, [1dc into next dc, 1dc into sp] 4 times, 1dc into next dc, turn, 10ch, miss 7dc, 1dc into next dc, 8ch, miss 1 picot, 1dc into next picot, 1ch, 1dc into next picot, 8ch miss 2 free picots, 1dc into next picot, turn, *[2dc, 1 picot] 4 times and 2dc* into next 8ch arch, 1dc into chsp, work * to * into each of next 2 arches, [2dc, 1 picot] twice into next arch, turn, 7ch, miss 4dc, 1dc into next dc, turn, [2dc, 1 picot] into last 7ch arch formed, turn, [8ch, miss 2 picots, 1dc into next picot, 1ch, 1dc into next picot] twice, 7ch, miss 4dc, 1dc into next dc, turn, [2dc, 1 picot] twice into last 7ch arch formed, turn, 8ch, miss 2 picots, 1dc into next picot, 1ch, 1dc into next picot, 8ch, 1dc into joining picot, 2ch, 1dc into next picot, turn, [1 picot, 2dc] into 2chsp, **work * to * into next 8ch arch, 1dc into chsp, * to * into next arch**, [2dc, 1 picot] twice and 2dc into next arch, 1dc into next sp; rep from ** to ** once more, 8ch, sl st into chsp on filling motif, turn,

21 If white is too stark for your taste, ecru is a warmer alternative, and is a practical choice for the muted beauty of this intricate kitchen curtain.

work * to * into last 8ch arch formed, turn, [2dc, 1 picot] twice and 2dc into next arch, 1dc into picot of filling motif, sl st to 8ch arch at left of 5-picot arch, then complete the arch by working [2dc, 1 picot] twice and 2dc into it. Fasten off.

Work other top corner to match.

Top Edge Filling Arches

With wrong side facing rejoin yarn with a dc into joining picot between 2 motifs, 8ch, miss 1 picot, [1dc into next picot 1ch] 4 times, 1dc into next picot, 8ch, 1dc into joining picot between 2 motifs, turn, [2dc, 1 picot, 2dc, 1 joining picot into filling motif, 2dc, joining picot into next picot 2dc, 1 picot, 2dc] into last 8ch arch formed, 1dc into next dc, turn, 8ch, miss 1 picot, 1dc in next picot, turn, * [2dc, 1 picot] 4 times and 2dc* into last 8ch arch formed, 1dc

into next dc, [1dc into next sp, 1dc into next dc] 4 times, turn, 10ch, miss 8dc, 1dc into next dc, turn; rep from * to * once into last 10ch arch formed, [2dc, 1 picot, 2dc] into next arch, turn, 7ch, miss 5dc, 1dc into next dc turn, [2dc, 1 picot, 2dc] into last arch formed, turn, 8ch, miss 3 picots, 1dc between 2 picots, 8ch, miss 3 picots, 1dc into next picot, 1ch, 1dc into next picot, 8ch, miss 2 picots, 1dc into 2nd dc, turn; rep from * to * into last 8ch arch formed, 2dc into next sp; rep from * to * into each of next 2 arches, 8ch, sl st into chsp of next filling motif, turn; rep from * to * into last arch formed, turn, [1 picot, 2dc] twice into next arch, 1 joining picot into 2nd picot of large motif, 2dc, 1 joining picot into 3rd picot of motif, 2dc, 1 picot, 2dc. Fasten off.

Work in between remaining motifs in the same way.

22

Hexagonal Star Motif

✪✪

Materials

Coats Patons Musica No. 5 Crochet Cotton Shade 500 - 50 grams

1.75mm Milward Steel Crochet Hook

Special Abbreviation

Popcorn = Work 7tr into next st or space, drop loop from hook, insert hook from the front into the top of first of these tr, pick up dropped loop and draw through tr.

To Make

Make 7ch, join into a ring with a sl st.

1st round: 3ch, work 17tr into ring, sl st into 3rd of 3ch.

2nd round: 3ch (count as 1tr), [1tr, 2ch, 2tr] into next st, *3ch, miss 2 sts, [2tr, 2ch, 2tr] into next st; rep from * 4 times, 3ch, miss 2 sts, sl st into 3rd of 3ch.

3rd round: Sl st to first sp, 3ch, [1tr, 2ch, 2tr] into same sp as last sl st, *3ch, 1 popcorn into next sp, 3ch [2tr, 2ch, 2tr] into next sp; rep from * 4 times, 3ch, 1 popcorn into next sp, 3ch, sl st into 3rd of 3ch.

4th round: Sl st to first sp, 3ch, [1tr, 2ch, 2tr] into same sp as last sl st, *3ch, [1 popcorn into next sp, 3ch] twice [2tr, 2ch, 2tr] into next sp; rep from * 4 times, 3ch, [1 popcorn into next sp, 3ch] twice sl st into 3rd of 3ch.

5th round: Sl st to first sp, 3ch, [1tr, 2ch, 2tr] into same sp as last sl st, *3ch, [1 popcorn into next sp, 3ch] 3 times, [2tr, 2ch, 2tr] into next sp; rep from * 4 times, 3ch, [1 popcorn into next sp, 3ch] 3 times, sl st into 3rd of 3ch.

6th round: Sl st to first sp, 3ch, [1tr, 2ch, 2tr] into same sp as last sl st, *3ch, [1 popcorn into next sp, 3ch] 4 times, [2tr, 2ch, 2tr] into next sp; rep from * 4 times, 3ch, [1 popcorn into next sp, 3ch] 4 times, sl st into 3rd of 3ch.

7th round: Sl st to first sp, 3ch, [1tr, 2ch, 2tr] into same sp as last sl st, *3ch, [1 popcorn into next sp, 3ch] 5 times, [2tr, 2ch, 2tr] into next sp; rep from * 4 times, 3ch, [1 popcorn into next sp, 3ch] 5 times, sl st into 3rd of 3ch.

8th round: Sl st to first sp, 3ch, [1tr, 2ch, 2tr] into same sp as last sl st, *3ch, [1 popcorn into next sp, 3ch] 6 times, [2tr, 2ch, 2tr] into next sp; rep from * 4 times, 3ch, [1 popcorn into next sp, 3ch] 6 times, sl st into 3rd of 3ch.

9th round: Sl st to first sp, 3ch, [1tr, 2ch, 2tr] into same sp as last sl st, *3ch, 1tr into next sp, 3ch, [1 popcorn into next sp, 3ch] 5 times, 1tr into next sp, 3ch, [2tr, 2ch, 2tr] into next sp; rep from * 4 times, 3ch, 1tr into next sp, 3ch, [1 popcorn into next sp, 3ch] 5 times, 1tr into next sp, 3ch, sl st into 3rd of 3ch.

10th round: Sl st to first sp, 3ch, [1tr, 2ch, 2tr] into same sp as last sl st, *[3ch, 1tr into next arch] twice, [3ch, 1 popcorn into next sp] 4 times, [3ch, 1tr into next arch] twice, 3ch, [2tr, 2ch, 2tr] into next sp; rep from * 4 times, [3ch, 1tr into next arch] twice, [3ch, 1 popcorn into next sp] 4 times, 3ch, [1tr into next arch, 3ch] twice, sl st into 3rd of 3ch.

11th round: Sl st to first sp, 3ch, [1tr, 2ch, 2tr] into same sp as last sl st, *[3ch, 1tr into next arch] 3 times, [3ch, 1 popcorn into next sp] 3 times, [3ch, 1tr into next arch] 3 times, 3ch, [2tr, 2ch, 2tr] into next sp; rep from * 4 times, [3ch, 1tr into next arch] 3 times, [3ch, 1 popcorn into next sp] 3 times, 3ch, [1tr into next arch, 3ch] 3 times, sl st into 3rd of 3ch.

12th round: Sl st to first sp, 3ch, [1tr, 2ch, 2tr] into same sp as last sl st, *[3ch, 1tr into next arch] 4 times, [3ch, 1 popcorn into next sp] twice, [3ch, 1tr into next arch] 4 times, 3ch, [2tr, 2ch, 2tr] into next sp; rep from * 4 times, [3ch, 1tr into next arch] 4 times, [3ch, 1 popcorn into next sp] twice, 3ch, [1tr into next arch, 3ch] 4 times, sl st into 3rd of 3ch.

13th round: Sl st to first sp, 3ch, [1tr, 2ch, 2tr] into same sp as last sl st, *3ch, [1tr into next arch, 3ch] 5 times, 1 popcorn into next sp, 3ch, [1tr into next arch, 3ch] 5 times, [2tr, 2ch, 2tr] into next sp; rep from * 4 times, 3ch, [1tr into next arch, 3ch] 5 times, 1 popcorn into next sp, 3ch, [1tr into next arch, 3ch] 5 times, sl st into 3rd of 3ch.

14th round: Sl st to first sp, 3ch, [1tr, 2ch, 2tr] into same sp as last sl st, *3ch, [1tr into next arch, 3ch] 12 times, [2tr, 2ch, 2tr] into next sp; rep from * 4 times, 3ch, [1tr into next arch, 3ch] 12 times, sl st into 3rd of 3ch.

15th round: Sl st to first sp, 3ch, [1tr, 2ch, 2tr] into same sp as last sl st, *3ch, [1tr into next sp, 3ch] 13 times, [2tr, 2ch, 2tr] into next sp; rep from * 4 times, 3ch, [1tr into next sp, 3ch] 13 times, sl st into 3rd of 3ch.

16th round: 1dc into each of first 2tr, *4dc into next arch, 1dc into each of next 2tr, [2dc into next arch, 1dc into next tr] 13 times, 2dc into next arch, 1dc into each of next 2tr; rep from * to end omitting 2dc at end of last rep, sl st into first dc.

Fasten off.

JUST WHITE

We've based the next few patterns on old-fashioned designs for a trousseau, but you don't have to wait for a wedding to make them. All of them can be used to build up wonderful bedspreads or cushions.

23

23

Square Motif with Star

✪✪

Materials

Coats Patons Musica No. 5 Crochet Cotton Shade 500 - 50 grams

1.75mm Milward Steel Crochet Hook

Special Abbreviations

1 corner = 2tr into 2chsp, 2ch [2tr, 3ch, 2tr] into 3chsp, 2ch, 2tr into 2chsp.

Bobble = Work 6dtr into next st or space as indicated until 1 loop of each dtr remains on hook, yo and through all 7 loops. Note: If bobbles tend to go at back of work (wrong side), push them to the front as you go along.

Note

All stitches are to be worked in the back loop only, to give the relief effect.

To Make

Make 12ch, join into a ring with a sl st.

1st round: Work 16dc into ring, sl st into first dc.

2nd round: 4ch (count as 1tr, 1ch), miss first dc, *1tr into next dc, 1ch; rep from * to end, sl st into 3rd of 4ch.

3rd round: 5ch (count as 1tr, 2ch), miss first tr, *1tr into next tr, 2ch; rep from * to end, sl st into 3rd of 5ch.

4th round: 4ch, *1 bobble into next sp, 1ch, 1tr into next tr; rep from * to last sp, 1 bobble into last sp, 1ch, sl st into 3rd of 4ch.

5th round: Sl st to top of next bobble, 3ch (count as 1tr), [1 bobble, 1tr, 1ch] into top of same bobble, [1tr, 1 bobble, 1tr, 1ch] into each of next 3 bobbles, 9ch, *[1tr, 1 bobble, 1tr, 1ch] into each of next 4 bobbles, 9ch; rep from * twice more, sl st into 3rd of 3ch.

6th round: Sl st to next chsp, 3ch, [1 bobble, 1tr, 1ch] into same sp, [1tr, 1 bobble, 1tr, 1ch into next chsp] twice, 1ch, [3tr, 2ch, 2tr, 3ch, 2tr, 2ch, 3tr, 2ch] into 9chsp, *[1tr, 1 bobble, 1tr, 1ch into next chsp] 3 times, 1ch, [3tr, 2ch, 2tr,

3ch, 2tr, 2ch, 3tr, 2ch] into 9chsp; rep from * twice more, sl st into 3rd of 3ch.

7th round: Sl st to next chsp, 3ch, [1 bobble, 1tr, 1ch] into same sp, [1tr, 1 bobble, 1tr, 2ch] into next chsp, 2tr into 2chsp, 1tr into each of next 3tr, 1 corner, 1tr into each of next 3tr, 3tr, 2tr in 2chsp, 2ch, *[1tr, 1 bobble, 1tr, 1ch into next chsp] twice, 1ch, 2tr in 2chsp, 1tr into each of next 3tr, 1 corner, 1tr into each of next 3tr, 2tr into 2chsp, 2ch; rep from * twice, sl st into 3rd of 3ch.

8th round: Sl st to next chsp, 3ch, [1 bobble, 1tr, 2ch] into same sp, 2tr into 2chsp, 7tr, 1 corner, 7tr, 2tr into 2chsp, 2ch, *[1tr, 1 bobble, 1tr, 2ch] into next chsp, 2tr into 2chsp, 7tr, 1 corner, 7tr, 2tr into 2chsp, 2ch; rep from * twice, sl st into 3rd of 3ch.

9th round: 3ch, 1tr into top of bobble, 1tr into next tr, 2tr into 2chsp, 11tr, 1 corner, *11tr, 2tr into 2chsp, 1tr into each of next 3 sts, 2tr into 2chsp, 11tr, 1 corner; rep from * twice, 11tr, 2tr into 2chsp, 8tr, sl st into 3rd of 3ch.

10th round: 3ch, 17tr, 1 corner, *33tr, 1 corner; rep from * twice, 15tr, sl st into 3rd of 3ch.

11th round: 3ch, 19tr, 1 corner, *37tr, 1 corner; rep from * twice, 17tr, sl st into 3rd of 3ch.

12th round: 3ch, 21tr, 1 corner, *41tr, 1 corner; rep from * twice, 19tr, sl st into 3rd of 3ch.

Fasten off.

24
Cross and Diamond Square

✪

Materials

Coats Patons Opera No. 20 Crochet Cotton Shade 500 - 50 grams
1.00mm Milward Steel Crochet Hook

Special Abbreviation

Bobble = Work 7dtr into next st or space as indicated until 1 loop of each

24

dtr remains on hook, yo and through all 8 loops. Note: If bobbles tend to go at back of work (wrong side), push them to the front as you go along.

To Make

Make 9ch, join into a ring with a sl st.

1st round: Work 16dc into ring, sl st into first dc.

2nd round: 3ch, 1tr, 3ch, *tr2tog, 3ch; rep from * 6 times, sl st into first dc.

3rd round: Sl st into first sp, 3ch (count as 1tr), 2tr into same sp as sl st, *2ch, [2tr, 3ch, 2tr] into next sp, 2ch, 3tr into next sp; rep from * to end omitting 3tr at end of last rep, sl st into 3rd of 3ch.

4th round: 3ch (count as 1tr), 1tr into each of next 2tr, *2tr into 2chsp, 2ch, [2tr, 3ch, 2tr] into 3chsp, 2ch, 2tr into 2chsp, 1tr into each of next 3tr; rep from * to end omitting 3tr at end of last rep, sl st into 3rd of 3ch.

5th round: 3ch, 1tr into each of next 4tr, *2tr into 2chsp, 2ch, [2tr, 3ch, 2tr] into 3chsp, 2ch, 2tr into 2chsp, 1tr into each of next 7tr; rep from * to end omitting 5tr at end of last rep, sl st into 3rd of last 3ch.

6th round: 3ch, *1 bobble into next st, 1tr into each of next 5tr, 2tr into 2chsp, 2ch, [2tr, 3ch, 2tr] into 3chsp, 2ch, 2tr into 2chsp, 1tr into each of next 5tr; rep from * to end omitting 1tr at end of last rep, sl st into 3rd of last 3ch.

Working 1tr into each tr unless otherwise indicated, continue as follows:

7th round: 3ch, 2tr, *1 bobble, 5tr, 2tr into 2chsp, 2ch, [2tr, 3ch, 2tr] into 3chsp, 2ch, 2tr into 2chsp, 5tr, 1 bobble, 3tr; rep from * to end omitting 3tr at end of last rep, sl st into 3rd of last 3ch.

8th round: 3ch, *1 bobble, 3tr, 1 bobble, 5tr, 2tr into 2chsp, 2ch, [2tr, 3ch, 2tr] into 3chsp, 2ch, 2tr into 2chsp, 5tr, 1 bobble, 3tr; rep from * to end omitting 1tr at end of last rep, sl st into 3rd of 3ch.

9th round: 3ch, 2tr, *1 bobble, 3tr, 1 bobble, 5tr, 2tr into 2chsp, 2ch, [2tr, 3ch, 2tr] into 3chsp, 2ch, 2tr into 2chsp, 5tr, [1 bobble, 3tr] twice; rep from * to end omitting 1tr at end of last rep, sl st into 3rd of last 3ch.

10th round: 3ch, *[1 bobble, 3tr] twice, 1 bobble, 2tr, 2tr into 2chsp, 2ch, [2tr, 3ch, 2tr] into 3chsp, 2ch, 2tr into 2chsp, 2tr, 1 bobble, 3tr, 1 bobble, 3tr; rep from * to end omitting 1tr at end of last rep, sl st into 3rd of last 3ch.

11th round: 3ch, 2tr, *[1 bobble, 3tr] twice, 1 bobble, 5tr, 2tr into 2chsp, 2ch, [2tr, 3ch, 2tr] into 3chsp, 2ch, 2tr into 2chsp, 5tr, [1 bobble, 3tr] 3 times; rep from * to end omitting 1tr at end of last rep, sl st into 3rd of last 3ch.

12th round: 3ch, *[1 bobble, 3tr] twice, 1 bobble, 9tr, 2tr into 2chsp, 2ch, [2tr, 3ch, 2tr] into 3chsp, 2ch, 2tr into 2chsp, 9tr, 1 bobble, 3tr, 1 bobble, 3tr; rep from * to end omitting 1tr, at end of last rep, sl st into 3rd of 3ch.

13th round: 3ch, 2tr, *1 bobble, 3tr, 1 bobble, 13tr, 2tr into 2chsp, 2ch, [2tr, 3ch, 2tr] into 3chsp, 2ch, 2tr into 2chsp, 13tr, [1 bobble, 3tr] twice; rep from * to end omitting 1tr, at end of last rep, sl st into 3rd of 3ch.

14th round: 3ch, *1 bobble, 3tr, 1 bobble, 17tr, 2tr into 2chsp, 2ch, [2tr, 3ch, 2tr] into 3chsp, 2ch, 2tr into 2chsp, 17tr, 1 bobble, 2tr; rep from * to end omitting 1tr at end of last rep, sl st into 3rd of 3ch.

15th round: 3ch, 2tr, *1 bobble, 21tr, 2tr into 2chsp, 2ch, [2tr, 3ch, 2tr] into 3chsp, 2ch, 2tr into 2chsp, 21tr, 1 bobble, 3tr; rep from * to end omitting 3tr at end of last rep, sl st into 3rd of 3ch.

16th round: 3ch, *1 bobble, 25tr, 2tr into 2chsp, 2ch, [2tr, 3ch, 2tr] into 3chsp, 2ch, 2tr into 2chsp, 25tr; rep from * to end omitting 1tr at end of last rep, sl st into 3rd of 3ch.

17th round: 3ch, 28tr, *2tr into 2chsp, 2ch, [2tr, 3ch, 2tr] into 3chsp, 2ch, 2tr into 2chsp, 55tr; rep from * 4 times, 26tr, sl st into 3rd of 3ch.

18th round: 3ch, 30tr, *2tr into 2chsp, 2ch, [2tr, 3ch, 2tr] into 3chsp, 2ch, 2tr into 2chsp, 59tr; rep from * 4 times, 28tr, sl st into 3rd of 3ch.

19th round: 3ch, 32tr, *2tr into 2chsp, 2ch, [2tr, 3ch, 2tr] into 3chsp, 2ch, 2tr into 2chsp, 63tr; rep from * 4 times, 30tr, sl st into 3rd of 3ch.

Fasten off.

TIP

Before starting any crochet work make sure that your hands are scrupulously clean. Remember to check them whilst you are working, particularly if your hands are inclined to perspire a little.

25

Hexagonal Motif with Leaves

✪✪✪

Materials

Coats Patons Opera No. 5 Crochet Cotton Shade 500 - 50 grams

1.75mm Milward Steel Crochet Hook

Special Abbreviation

Bobble = Work 7dtr into next st or space as indicated until 1 loop of each dtr remains on hook, yo and through all 8 loops. Note: If bobbles tend to go at back of work (wrong side), push them to the front as you go along.

Note

Work all stitches into the **back loop** only.

Centre

Make 8ch, join into a ring with a sl st.

1st round: Work 12dc into ring, sl st into first dc.

2nd round: 3ch (count as 1tr), *[1 bobble, 1tr] into next st, 1tr into next st; rep from * 4 times, [1 bobble, 1tr] into next st, sl st into 3rd of 3ch.

3rd round: 1dc into each tr and 2dc into each bobble to end, sl st into first dc, (24 sts).

4th round: 3ch, *[1 bobble, 1tr] into next st, 1tr into next st; rep from * 10 times, [1 bobble, 1tr] into next st, sl st into 3rd of 3ch.

5th round: 1dc into each tr and 2dc into each bobble to end, sl st into first dc, (48 sts).

Fasten off.

Leaf

Make 8ch.

1st round: 1dc into 2nd ch from hook, 1dc into each of next 5ch, 3dc into last ch, do not turn but working on other side of starting ch work 1dc into each of next 6ch, 2dc into last ch, sl st into first dc, (16dc).

2nd round: 1dc into same st as last sl st, 1dc into each of next 6dc, 3dc into next dc, 1dc into each of next 8dc, sl st into first dc.

Work 2nd round twice more, but joining leaf to a popcorn with a sl st at end of last round.

Fasten off.

Work a further 11 leaves joining each one to a popcorn as before.

Border

Join yarn to tip of any leaf.

1st round: *1dc into tip of leaf, 11ch; rep from * to end, sl st into first dc.

2nd round: *11dc into next chsp, 3dc into next dc; rep from * to end, sl st into first dc.

3rd round: 1dc into each of first 12 sts, 3dc into next st, *1dc into each of next 25 sts, 3dc into next st; rep from * 4 times, 1dc into each of next 12 sts, sl st into first dc.

4th round: 1dc into each of first 13dc, 3dc into next st, *1dc into each of next 27dc, 3dc into next st; rep from * 4 times, 1dc into each of next 13dc, sl st into first dc.

5th round: 1dc into each of first 14dc, 3dc into next st, *1dc into each of next 29dc, 3dc into next st; rep from * 4 times, 1dc into each of next 14dc, sl st into first dc.

6th round: 4ch, work 6dtr into same st as last sl st until 1 loop of each dtr remains on hook, yo and through all 7 loops (1 bobble at beginning of round worked), 1tr into next st, [3ch, miss 3 sts, 1tr into next st, 1 bobble, 1tr into next st] twice, 7ch, miss 5sts, [1tr, into next st, 1 bobble, 1tr into next st, 3ch, miss 3sts] twice, 1tr into next st; rep from * to end omitting 1tr at end of last rep, sl st into 3rd of 3ch.

7th round: *1dc into each st to corner st, 3dc into corner st; rep from * 5 times, 1dc into each st to end, sl st into first dc.

8th round: 3ch (count as 1tr), *[1 bobble, 1tr into each of next 2 sts] 6 times, 3ch, miss 1 st, [1tr into each of next 2 sts, 1 bobble] 5 times, 1tr into each of next 2 sts; rep from * to end omitting 1tr at end of last rep, sl st into 3rd of 3ch.

9th round: As 7th round.

10th round: 3ch, *[1 bobble, 2tr] 6 times, 1 bobble, 1tr, 3ch, miss 1 st, 1tr, [1 bobble, 2tr] 6 times; rep from * to end omitting 1tr at end of last rep, sl st into 3rd of 3ch.

11th round: As 7th round.

Fasten off.